Table of Content

Foreword

Full stack developers top the list of best tech jobs in the U.S in terms of salary, number of job posts, and opportunities for growth. They are also one of the hardest to fill tech positions. With an average base salary of $111,640, companies that are investing in this position want to make sure they bring the right candidate on board.

"When I ask interview questions, I am not looking for a particular answer or expertise in each one" said John Maglione, senior talent acquisition specialist at WWT Asynchrony Labs. "Rather, these questions help me gain a solid understanding of where the candidate may be experience-wise with relation to the length of their career, because tenure, doesn't always translate to a deeper understanding of the discipline."

Full stack engineering interviews consist primarily of technical questions. Because full stack developers work with both back-end and front-end code, you should feel comfortable working with a variety of languages and answering questions ranging from databases and web servers to HMTL and UI implementation.

As such, you are also responsible for developing and designing application architecture, developing server side applications and working alongside graphic designers when implementing web designs, among other duties.

Candidates should also demonstrate good organizational skills and attention to detail. Bad candidates will lack interpersonal skills and struggle to communicate effectively. Treat your non technical abilities as equally important.

Before we start, let's lay down what will be covered in this book.

Part I goes through technical areas brought up during most software developer interview. We will discuss Object Oriented Programming, algorithms, databases, networking, security, and front end with HTML, CSS and Javascript.

Don't worry, you don't need to be an expert in all those fields and know every programming languages illustrated in the typical interview questions. What's important is to grasp the fundamentals and basic concepts to demonstrate familiarity with the full stack.

Part II covers the non technical aspects. Hiring managers are not generally looking for a coding guru. They are after the candidate who can show interpersonal skills, an attitude that will fit within the existing team, and someone they actually want to work with. Also, to get an interview, you first need to be called for one! The non technical part will detail steps to create the perfect resume and cover letter.

At the end of the book, you will find an Interview Cheat Sheet, it condenses all the do's and dont's to keep in mind before, during, and after the interview.

How to use this book

I remember struggling in front of the white board for two hours and walking out of the room not only mentally tired, but also devastated knowing I had missed out on a great opportunity due to lack of proper preparation. I swore I would never let it happen again, and I haven't.

I have worked as a Software Engineer for over 12 years, done server and web application development along with mobile app design and implementation. My experience across multiple industries, through coding, testing and architecturing distributed software systems thought me one thing: Being a *so called* full stack developer demands a broader set of computer skills than ever before.

From having participated in dozens of technical interviews with many software companies, and from conducting probably over a hundred interviews where I work(ed), the methodology followed by this book has been defined with the help of other experienced engineers and seasoned technical interviewers. Follow this, and you will absolutely crush most code-intensive tech interviews.

Assumptions

First and foremost, you already know how to code. You may or may not have a Computer Science background, that's OK, but you're already a decent coder, you just need a CS refresher, and a game plan for the interview day.

This book is a coding interview blue-print. You are, of course, expected to study and be prepared for other technology specific questions relevant to the job you intend to apply for. Such specific fields might be embedded computer systems, mobile app development, data science and data mining.

What to study

In nearly all interviews I've been through, I was questioned on General Programming principles, Binary Trees, Arrays and Linked Lists. Make sure to study and practice at large those topics which are presented in the first two chapters. No matter the job you are after, be well prepared for those.

The back end flavour

Job descriptions easily gives away the software developer profile companies are looking for. If the terms *OOP, Functional programming, Databases, Cloud computing* appear, you then need to master the concepts of Programming Principles, Algorithms, Databases, Security and Networking. Study those chapters in depth.

Continue your study by going through the HTML/CSS and JavaScript chapters, good chances are you will be quizzed on a few general front end concepts.

The front end flavour

If the required skills section mentions *solid web development knowledge, understanding of UI/UX, HTML, CSS and JS*, then your front end developement aptitudes are more relevant for the job. Study at large the HTML/CSS and JavaScript chapters.

Follow on by walking through all the other technical chapters.

Mock the interview

Use a white board or a pencil and paper. Follow this rule, and you'll be successful. Violate it at your own peril.

In the interview setting, you won't necessarily be given the comfort of using an IDE and compiler, so prepare in the most realistic way possible.

Eat the elephant one bite at a time

The topic of computer science is very dense, and some subject matters can be hard to digest, chapter 2 on Algorithms particularly is. Pick a particular area, increasing the difficulty as you go, and try to solve 4 to 8 coding questions per day. Anymore than this, and you may start to lose your drive to study, begin skipping days, and your study plan will slowly unravel.

Dedicate one day to reviewing that week's questions and study topics. This is extremely important for material retention. Take one day off per week to give your brain a break. This is important, everyone needs to rest and relax.

Let's say you devote 6 weeks to interview preparation. At 6 days per week, with 1 day dedicated to review, that gives 5 days a week for coding questions. You're going to solve 120 questions - assuming 4 questions per day, or 240 questions - assuming 8 questions per day. That's pretty serious progress, and 6 weeks will go by in a blur!

Don't cram, unless absolutely necessary! Re-read the section on properly preparing if needed. A crash course will yield marginal results at best, failure at worst.

Leetcode

Leetcode has hundreds of practical questions and solutions, this should be your absolute destination for practicing programming questions and code katas.

Many of the commonly algorithm interview questions covered in this book contain references to Leetcode exercises, I encourage you to go through as many of them possible to master your algorithm skills.

PART I - Technical

This part covers the technical topics to prepare for your technical interviews. Programming principles, algorithms, databases, networking and security are subjects that usually come up for any software developer role. It follows up with HTML5/CSS and JavaScript topics, technologies that are becoming utmost important for full stack developer jobs.

The more fields and techniques you have in your arsenal, the higher the chances of passing the interview. Even for a seasoned software developer, those chapters may lead you to discover information and corner cases you might have missed out.

Chapter 1 - Programming Principles

General programming concepts are important to understand. Most interviewers will only ask a handful of Computer Science fundamental questions, but it is important to be ready for them and know how to legibly answer them.

Object Oriented Programming

What is Object Oriented Programming?

Object Oriented Programming (OOP) is a programming paradigm where the complete software operates as a series of objects talking to each other. An object is a collection of data and methods that operate on its data.

What are the advantages of OOP?

The main advantage of OOP is better manageable code that covers following:

1. The overall understanding of the software increases as the distance between the language spoken by developers and that spoken by users.
2. Object orientation eases maintenance by the use of encapsulation. One can easily change the underlying representation by keeping the methods same. OOP paradigm is mainly useful for relatively big software.

What are the main features of OOP?

- Encapsulation
- Polymorphism
- Inheritance

What is a class?

A class is a representation of a type of object. It is the blueprint/plan/template that describes the details of an object.

What is an object?

An object is an instance of a class. It has its own state, behavior, and identity.

What is a constructor?

A constructor is a method used to initialize the state of an object, and it gets invoked at the time of object creation. Rules for a constructor are:

1. Constructor name should be the same as its class name.
2. A constructor must have no return type.

What are the various types of constructors?

There are three various types of constructors, and they are as follows:

1. Default Constructor – Has no parameters.
2. Parametric Constructor – Has a one more parameters. Creates a new instance of a class given the passed parameters.
3. Copy Constructor – Creates a new object as a copy of an existing object.

What is 'this'?

this refers to the current object of a class. this keyword is used as a pointer which differentiates between the given object and the global object. Basically, it refers to the current object.

What is method overloading?

Method overloading is the concept of creating several methods having the same name but differ from each other by the type and/or number of input parameters taken.

Examples:

```
void add(int a, int b);
void add(double a, double b);
void add(String a, String b);
void add(int a, int b, int c);
```

Difference between overloading and overriding?

Overloading is static binding whereas Overriding is dynamic binding. Overloading is nothing but the same method with different arguments, and it may or may not return the same value in the same class itself.

Overriding is the same method names with same arguments associated with the class and its child class.

What are access modifiers?

Access modifiers determine the scope of the method or variables that can be accessed from other various objects or classes.

What is exception handling?

An exception is an event that occurs during the execution of a program. Many exceptions types exist – Runtime exception, Error exceptions, etc. Those exceptions are adequately handled through exception handling mechanism using the *try, catch* and *throw* keywords.

What is encapsulation?

Encapsulation refers to one of the following two notions.

1. Data hiding: A language feature to restrict access to members of an object. For example, private and protected members in C++.
2. Bundling of data and methods together: Data and methods that operate on that data are bundled together.

What is Polymorphism?

Polymorphism means that some code or operations or objects behave differently in different contexts.

What is Inheritance? What is its purpose?

The idea of inheritance is that a class (called child or sub class) is based on another class (parent or super class) and uses data and implementation of that other class. The purpose of inheritance is code/logic reuse.

What is the difference between an interface and an abstract class?

Abstract Class

- For an abstract class, a method must be declared as abstract. An abstract method doesn't have an implementation.

- The Abstract methods can be declared with Access modifiers like public, internal, protected, etc. When implementing these methods in a subclass, you must define them with the same (or a less restricted) visibility.
- Abstract classes can contain variables and concrete methods.
- A class can Inherit only one Abstract class. Hence multiple inheritance is not possible for an Abstract class.
- Abstract is object-oriented. It offers the basic data an 'object' should have and/or functions it should be able to do. It is concerned with the object's basic characteristics: what it has and what it can do. Hence objects which inherit from the same abstract class share the basic characteristics (generalization).
- Abstract class establishes "is a" relation with concrete classes.

Interface

- For an interface, all the methods are abstract by default. So one cannot declare variables or concrete methods in interfaces.
- All methods declared in an interface must be public.
- Interfaces cannot contain variables and concrete methods except constants.
- A class can implement many interfaces. Hence multiple interface inheritance is possible.
- Interface is functionality-oriented. It defines functionalities an object should have. Regardless what object it is, as long as it can do these functionalities, which are defined in the interface, it's fine. It ignores everything else. An object/class can contain several (groups of) functionalities; hence it is possible for a class to implement multiple interfaces.
- Interface provides "has a" capability for classes.

Typical Object-Oriented Programming Challenges

- How would you design a chess game? What classes and objects would you use? What methods would they have?
- How would you design the data structures of book keeping system for a library?
- Explain how you would design an HTTP server? Give examples of classes, methods, and interfaces. What are the challenges here?
- Discuss algorithms and data structures for a garbage collector?
- How would you implement an HR system to keep track of employee salaries and benefits?

Functional Programming

What is functional programming?

Functional programming produces programs by composing mathematical functions and avoids shared state & mutable data. Lisp (specified in 1958) was among the first languages to support functional programming and was heavily inspired by lambda calculus. Lisp and many Lisp family languages are still in everyday use today.

Functional programming is an essential concept in JavaScript, it is declarative rather than imperative, and application state flows through pure functions. Contrast with object oriented programming, where application state is usually shared and colocated with methods in objects.

Functional code tends to be more concise, more predictable, and easier to test than imperative or object oriented code.

What is a Pure Function?

A pure function is a function which:

- Given the same inputs, always returns the same output
- Has no side-effects
- Pure functions have lots of properties that are important in functional programming, including referential transparency.

What is the meaning of Side Effects?

A side effect is any application state change that is observable outside the called function other than its return value. Side effects include:

- Modifying any external variable or object property (e.g., a global variable, or a variable in the parent function scope chain)
- Logging to the console
- Writing to the screen

Side effects are mostly avoided in functional programming, which makes the effects of a program easier to understand and test.

What is Immutability?

An immutable object is an object that can't get its state modified after its creation.

What is a higher order function?

Higher order functions are functions that take a function as an argument, returns a function, or both. They are often used to:

- Abstract or isolate actions, effects, or async flow control using callback functions, promises, etc.
- Create utilities which can act on a wide variety of data types.
- Partially apply a function to its arguments or create a curried function for the purpose of reuse or function composition.
- Take a list of functions and return some composition of those input functions.

Curried Function, what is that?

A curried function is a function of several arguments rewritten in such a way that it accepts the first argument and returns a function that accepts the second argument and so on. This allows functions of several arguments to have some of their initial arguments partially applied.

For example, in JavaScript:

```
let add = function(x) {
  return function(y) {
    return x + y;
  };
};
```

Would allow us to call it like so:

```
let addTen = add(10);
```

When this runs, the value 10 is passed in as x;

```
let add = function(10) {
  return function(y) {
    return 10 + y;
  };
};
```

Calling addTen(4) returns 10 + 4.

Is Functionnal Programming Declarative or Imperative?

Functional programming is a declarative paradigm, meaning that the program logic is expressed without explicitly describing the flow control.

Imperative programs spend lines of code describing the specific steps used to achieve the desired results—the flow control: How to do things

Declarative programs abstract the flow control process, and instead spend lines of code describing the data flow: What to do. The how gets abstracted away.

Chapter 2 - Algorithms

Coding interviews often comprise of data structure and algorithm-based questions as well as some of the logical questions such as: *How do you swap two integers without using a temporary variable?*

This chapter deep dives into practical exercises, tips and typical interview questions on specific topics of algorithms and data structures. Many algorithm questions involve techniques that can be applied to questions of similar nature.

It is helpful to divide algorithm questions into different topic areas. The topic areas I've seen most often in interviews are array, linked list, string, binary tree.

It's not guaranteed that you will be asked very challenging coding or data structure and algorithmic questions, but this will give you enough of an idea of the kinds of questions you can expect.

By the way, the more questions you solve in practice, the better your preparation will be. Once you have gone through and practice these questions, you should feel confident enough to take on more abstract logical questions.

For each topic, a brief introduction is given, followed by online exercises to practice the topic on LeetCode. Free of use, the web interface allows you to edit and execute code online, and usually provides you with hints and solutions for each exercise. Further study links are recommended reading to help you fully understand each concept.

If you are reading this on the Kindle or got a hard copy, you can conveniently type this shortlink on your browser to see all the exercises and further reading reference links: https://bit.ly/2Eh45fM or https://tinyurl.com/yacn99hb

General Tips

Clarify any assumptions you made subconsciously. Many questions are under-specified on purpose.

Always validate input first. Check for invalid/empty/negative/different type input. Never assume you are given valid parameters. Alternatively, clarify with the interviewer whether you can assume valid input (usually yes), which can save you time from writing code that does input validation.

Are there any time/space complexity requirements/constraints? Check for off-by-one errors.

In languages where there are no automatic type coercion, check that concatenation of values are of the same type.

After finishing your code, use a few example inputs to test your solution.

Is the algorithm meant to be run multiple times, for example in a web server? If yes, the input is likely to be preprocess-able to improve the efficiency in each call.

Use a mix of functional and imperative programming paradigms:

- Write pure functions as much as possible.
- Pure functions are easier to reason about and can help to reduce bugs in your implementation.

- Avoid mutating the parameters passed into your function especially if they are passed by reference unless you are sure of what you are doing.
- However, functional programming is usually expensive in terms of space complexity because of non-mutation and the repeated allocation of new objects. On the other hand, imperative code is faster because you operate on existing objects. Hence you will need to achieve a balance between accuracy vs efficiency, by using the right amount of functional and imperative code where appropriate.
- Avoid relying on and mutating global variables. Global variables introduce state.
- If you have to rely on global variables, make sure that you do not mutate it by accident.

Generally, to improve the speed of a program, we can either: (1) choose a more appropriate data structure/algorithm; or (2) use more memory. The latter demonstrates a classic space vs. time tradeoff, but it is not necessarily the case that you can only achieve better speed at the expense of space. Also, note that there is often a theoretical limit to how fast your program can run (in terms of time complexity). For instance, a question that requires you to find the smallest/largest element in an unsorted array cannot run faster than $O(N)$.

Data structures are your weapons. Choosing the right weapon for the right battle is the key to victory. Be very familiar about the strengths of each data structure and the time complexities for its various operations.

Data structures can be augmented to achieve efficient time complexities across different operations. For example, a hash map can be used together with a doubly-linked list to achieve O(1) time complexity for both the get and put operation in an <u>LRU cache</u>.

Hashmaps are probably the most commonly used data structure for algorithm questions. If you are stuck on a question, your last resort can be to enumerate through the possible data structures (thankfully there aren't that many of them) and consider whether each of them can be applied to the problem. This has worked for me sometimes.

If you are cutting corners in your code, state that out loud to your interviewer and say what you would do in a non-interview setting (no time constraints). E.g: *I would write a regex to parse this string rather than using split() which may not cover all cases.*

Math & Binary

Math

If code involves division or modulo, remember to check for division or modulo by 0 case. When a question involves "a multiple of a number", perhaps modulo might be useful.

Check for and handle overflow/underflow if you are using a typed language like Java and C++. At the very least, mention that overflow/underflow is possible and ask whether you need to handle it.

Consider negative numbers and floating point numbers. This may sound obvious, but under interview pressure, many obvious cases go unnoticed.

If the question asks to implement an operator such as power, square root or division and want it to be faster than $O(n)$, binary search is usually the approach to go.

Some common formulas

- Sum of 1 to N = $(n+1) * n/2$
- Sum of GP = $2^0 + 2^1 + 2^2 + 2^3 + ... 2^n = 2^{n+1} - 1$
- Permutations of N = $N! / (N-K)!$
- Combinations of N = $N! / (K! * (N-K)!)$

Practice Math Online

- Pow(x, n)
- Sqrt(x)
- Integer to English Words

Typical Math Questions

1. Given a string such as "123" or "67", write a function to output the number represented by the string without using casting. ([Solution](#))
2. Make a program that can print out the text form of numbers from 1 to 9999 (ex. 20 is "twenty", 105 is "one hundred and five", 2655 is "two thousand six hundred fifty five"). ([Solution](#))
3. How would you convert Roman numerals into decimals? E.g. XIV becomes 14. ([Solution](#))
4. Compute the square root of an Integer without using any existing built in math functions. ([Solution](#))

Binary

Questions involving binary representations and bitwise operations are asked sometimes and you must be absolutely familiar with how to convert a number from decimal form into binary form (and vice versa) in your chosen programming language.

Some helpful utility snippets:

- Test k^{th} bit is set: num & (1 << k) != 0.
- Set k^{th} bit: num |= (1 << k).
- Turn off k^{th} bit: num &= ~(1 << k).
- Toggle the kth bit: num ^= (1 << k).
- To check if a number is a power of 2, num & num - 1 == 0.

Corner Cases

- Check for overflow/underflow.
- Negative numbers.

Practice Binary Online

- Sum of Two Integers
- Number of 1 Bits
- Counting Bits
- Missing Number
- Reverse Bits

Read Further Binary Study Online

- Bits, Bytes, Building With Binary

Typical Binary Interview Questions

1. How do you verify if an integer is a power of 2? (Solution)
2. Write a program to print the binary representation of an integer. (Solution)
3. Write a program to print out the number of 1 bits in a given integer. (Solution)
4. Write a program to determine the next higher integer using the same number of 1 bits in a given number. (Solution)

Sequences

Arrays and strings are considered sequences (a string is a sequence of characters). There are tips relevant for dealing with both arrays and strings which are covered in this topic.

General

Are there duplicate values in the sequence, would it affect the answer? Check for sequence out of bounds.

Be mindful about slicing or concatenating sequences in your code. Typically, slicing and concatenating sequences require O(n) time. Use start and end indices to demarcate a subarray/substring where possible.

Sometimes you can traverse the sequence from the right rather than from the left.

Master the sliding window technique that applies to many substring/subarray problems.

When you are given two sequences to process, it is common to have one index per sequence to traverse/compare them both. For example, we use that approach to merge two sorted arrays in one of the typical question.

Corner Cases

- Empty sequence.
- Sequence with 1 or 2 elements.

- Sequence with repeated elements.

Arrays

Is the array sorted or partially sorted? If it is, some form of binary search should be possible. It usually means that the interviewer is looking for a solution that is faster than $O(n)$.

Can you sort the array? Sometimes sorting the array first may significantly simplify the problem. Make sure that the order of array elements do not need to be preserved before attempting a sort.

For questions where summation or multiplication of a subarray is involved, pre-computation using hashing or a prefix/suffix sum/product might be useful.

If you are given a sequence and the interviewer asks for $O(1)$ space, it might be possible to use the array itself as a hash table. For example, if the array only has values from 1 to N, where N is the length of the array, negate the value at that index (minus one) to indicate presence of that number.

Practice Arrays Online

- Two Sum
- Best Time to Buy and Sell Stock
- Contains Duplicate
- Product of Array Except Self
- Maximum Subarray
- Maximum Product Subarray
- Find Minimum in Rotated Sorted Array
- Search in Rotated Sorted Array

- 3Sum
- Container With Most Water

Typical Arrays Interview Questions

1. Given an array and an index, find the product of the elements of the array except the element at that index. (Solution)
2. Given 2 separate arrays, write a method to find the values that exist in both arrays and return them. (Solution)
3. Given an array of numbers, list out all triplets that sum to 0. Do so with a running time of less than $O(n^3)$. (Solution 1)
4. Given an array of integers, find the subarray with the largest sum. (Solution)
5. Find the second maximum value in an array. (Solution)
6. Remove duplicates in an unsorted array where the duplicates are at a distance of k or less from each other. (Solution)
7. Given an unsorted list of integers, return true if the list contains any duplicates within k indices of each element. Do it faster than $O(n^2)$. (Solution)
8. Given an array of string, find the duplicated elements. (Solution)
9. Given an array of integers, modify the array by moving all the zeroes to the end (right side). The order of other elements doesn't matter. E.g. [1, 2, 0, 3, 0, 1, 2], the program could output [1, 2, 3, 1, 2, 0, 0]. (Solution)
10. Given an array of integers where every value appears twice except one, find the single, non-repeating value. Follow up: do so with O(1) space. E.g., [2, 5, 3, 2, 1, 3, 4, 5, 1] returns 4, because it is the only value that appears in the array only once. (Solution)

String

Please read the above tips on sequence. They apply to strings too.

Ask about input character set and case sensitivity. Usually the characters are limited to lowercase Latin characters, for example a to z.

When you need to compare strings where the order isn't important (like anagram), you may consider using a HashMap as a counter. If your language has a built-in Counter class like in Python, ask to use that instead.

If you need to keep a counter of characters, a common mistake is to say that the space complexity required for the counter is $O(n)$. The space required for a counter is $O(1)$ not $O(n)$. This is because the upper bound is the range of characters, which is usually a fixed constant of 26. The input set is just lowercase Latin characters.

Common data structures for looking up strings efficiently are

- Trie / Prefix Tree
- Suffix Tree

Trees are covered in the Sequence section later in this Chapter.

Common String algorithms

- Rabin Karp for efficient searching of substring using a rolling hash.
- KMP for efficient searching of substring.

Make sure to be familiar with those algorithms.

Corner Cases

- Strings with only one distinct character.

Non-repeating Characters

- Use a 26-bit bitmask to indicate which lower case latin characters are inside the string.

```
mask = 0
for c in set(word):
  mask |= (1 << (ord(c) - ord('a')))
```

To determine if two strings have common characters, perform & on the two bitmasks. If the result is non-zero, mask_a & mask_b > 0, then the two strings have common characters.

Anagram

An anagram is word switch or word play. It is the result of re-arranging the letters of a word or phrase to produce a new word or phrase, while using all the original letters only once. In interviews, usually we are only bothered with words without spaces in them.

To determine if two strings are anagrams, there are a few plausible approaches:

- Sorting both strings should produce the same resulting string. This takes O(nlgn) time and O(lgn) space.

- If we map each character to a prime number and we multiply each mapped number together, anagrams should have the same multiple (prime factor decomposition). This takes $O(n)$ time and $O(1)$ space.
- Frequency counting of characters will help to determine if two strings are anagrams. This also takes $O(n)$ time and $O(1)$ space.

Palindrome

A palindrome is a word, phrase, number, or other sequence of characters which reads the same backward as forward, such as *madam* or *racecar*.

Here are ways to determine if a string is a palindrome:

- Reverse the string and it should be equal to itself.
- Have two pointers at the start and end of the string. Move the pointers inward till they meet. At any point in time, the characters at both pointers should match.

The order of characters within the string matters, so HashMaps are usually not helpful.

When a question is about counting the number of palindromes, a common trick is to have two pointers that move outward, away from the middle. Note that palindromes can be even or odd length. For each middle pivot position, you need to check it twice: Once that includes the character and once without the character.

- For substrings, you can terminate early once there is no match.
- For subsequences, use dynamic programming as there are overlapping subproblems. Check out this

question.

Dynamic programming is further covered in this Chapter.

Practice String Online

- Longest Substring Without Repeating Characters
- Longest Repeating Character Replacement
- Minimum Window Substring
- Valid Anagram
- Group Anagrams
- Valid Parentheses
- Valid Palindrome
- Longest Palindromic Substring
- Palindromic Substrings

Typical String Interview Questions

1. Write a program that checks if a sentence is palindrome or not. You can ignore white spaces and other characters to consider sentence as a palindrome. (Solution)
2. Given a list of words, find if any of the two words can be joined to form a palindrome. (Solution)
3. Write a functions that returns true if edit distance between two strings is one. An edit is characterised by either a character add, remove, or change in the string. (Solution)
4. How would you define a spell-checking algorithm? (Solution)
5. Given a string, return the string with duplicate characters removed. (Solution)
6. Given a rectangular grid with letters, search if some word is in the grid. (Solution)
7. Given two numbers as strings. The numbers may be very large (may not fit in long long int), the task is to find the sum of these two numbers. (Solution)

8. Find the longest palindrome in a string. (Solution)
9. Check whether two strings are anagram of each other. (Solution)
10. Run length encoding - Given an input string, write a function that returns the Run Length Encoded string for the input string. For example, if the input string is "wwwwaaadexxxxxx", then the function should return "w4a3d1e1x6". (Solution)
11. Given a dictionary find out if given word can be made by two words in the dictionary. (Solution)

Interval

Interval questions are questions where you are given an array of two-element arrays (an interval) and the two values represent a start and an end value. Interval questions are considered part of the array family but they involve some common techniques hence they are extracted out to this special section of their own.

An example interval array: [[1, 2], [4, 7]].

Interval questions can be tricky to those who have not tried them before because of the sheer number of cases to consider when they overlap.

Do clarify with the interviewer whether [1, 2] and [2, 3] are considered overlapping intervals as it affects how you will write your equality checks.

A common routine for interval questions is to sort the array of intervals by each interval's starting value. Be familiar with writing code to check if two intervals overlap and merging two overlapping intervals:

```
def is_overlap(a, b):
  return a[0] < b[1]
        and
        b[0] < a[1]

def merge_overlapping_intervals(a, b):
  return [min(a[0], b[0]),
        max(a[1], b[1])
        ]
```

Corner Cases

- Single interval.
- Non-overlapping intervals.
- An interval totally consumed within another interval.
- Duplicate intervals.

Practice Interval Online

- Insert Interval
- Merge Intervals
- Non-overlapping Intervals

Typical Interval Interview questions

1. Consider a big party where a log register for guest's entry and exit times is maintained. Find the time at which there are maximum guests in the party. Note that entries in register are not in any order. (Solution)
2. Given a set of time intervals in any order, merge all overlapping intervals into one and output the result which should have only mutually exclusive intervals. Let the intervals be represented as pairs of integers for simplicity. (Solution)

3. Given a set of non-overlapping intervals and a new interval, insert the interval at correct position. If the insertion results in overlapping intervals, then merge the overlapping intervals. Assume that the set of non-overlapping intervals is sorted on the basis of start time, to find correct position of insertion. (Solution)

4. Given n appointments, find all conflicting appointments. e.g appointments: [1, 5] [3, 7], [2, 6], [10, 15], [5, 6], [4, 100] should output:

- [3,7] Conflicts with [1,5]
- [2,6] Conflicts with [1,5]
- [5,6] Conflicts with [3,7]
- [4,100] Conflicts with [1,5] (Solution)

Graphs

General

Be familiar with the various graph representations, graph search algorithms and their time and space complexities.

You can be given a list of edges and tasked to build your own graph from the edges to perform a traversal on. The common graph representations are:

- Adjacent matrix.
- Adjacent list.
- Hashmap of hashmaps.

A tree-like diagram could very well be a graph that allows for cycles and a naive recursive solution would not work. In that case you will have to handle cycles and keep a set of visited nodes when traversing.

Graph search algorithms

- **Common** - Breadth-first Search, Depth-first Search
- **Uncommon** - Topological Sort, Dijkstra's algorithm
- **Rare** - Bellman-Ford algorithm, Floyd-Warshall algorithm, Prim's algorithm, Kruskal's algorithm

In coding interviews, graphs are commonly represented as 2-D matrices where cells are the nodes and each cell can traverse to its adjacent cells (up/down/left/right). Hence it is important that you be familiar with traversing a 2-D matrix. When recursively traversing the matrix, always ensure that your next position is within the boundary of the matrix.

Corner Cases

- Empty graph.
- Graph with one or two nodes.
- Disjoint graphs.
- Graph with cycles.

Practice Graph Online

- Clone Graph
- Course Schedule
- Pacific Atlantic Water Flow
- Number of Islands
- Longest Consecutive Sequence

Read Further Graph Study Online

- From Theory To Practice: Representing Graphs
- Deep Dive Through A Graph: DFS Traversal
- Going Broad In A Graph: BFS Traversal

Typical Graph Interview Questions

1. Given a list of sorted words from an alien dictionary, find the order of the alphabet. (Solution)
2. Given a graph and two nodes, determine if there exists a path between them. (Solution)
3. Determine if a cycle exists in a directed graph. (Solution)

Matrix

A matrix is a 2-dimensional array. Questions involving matrices relate to graph traversal, but also dynamic programming which is covered later in this chapter.

For questions involving traversal, you almost always want to make a copy of the matrix with the same dimensions that is initialized to empty values to store the visited state.

Many grid-based games can be modeled as a matrix, such as Tic-Tac-Toe, Sudoku, Crossword, Connect 4, Battleship, etc. It is not uncommon to be asked to verify the winning condition of the game. For games like Tic-Tac-Toe, Connect 4 and Crosswords, where verification has to be done vertically and horizontally, one trick is to write code to verify the matrix for the horizontal cells, transpose the matrix and reuse the logic for horizontal verification to verify originally vertical cells (which are now horizontal).

Transposing a matrix in Python is simply:

```
transposed_matrix = zip(*matrix)
```

Corner Cases

- Empty matrix. Check that none of the arrays are 0 length.
- 1 x 1 matrix.
- Matrix with a single row or column.

Practice Matrix Online

- Set Matrix Zeroes
- Spiral Matrix
- Rotate Image
- Word Search

Typical Matrix Interview Questions

1. Given a 4 x 4 matrix, the task is to interchange the elements of the first and last column and show the

resulting matrix. (<u>Solution</u>)
2. Boggle implementation. Given a dictionary, and a matrix of letters, find all the words in the matrix that are in the dictionary. You can go across, down or diagonally. (<u>Solution</u>)
3. Given a 2D array, print it in spiral form. (<u>Solution</u>)

Linked List

Like arrays, linked lists are used to represent sequential data. The benefit of linked lists is that insertion and deletion from anywhere in the list is O(1) whereas in arrays the following elements will have to be shifted.

Adding a dummy node at the head and/or tail might help to handle many edge cases where operations have to be performed at the head or the tail. The presence of dummy nodes essentially ensures that operations will never have be done on the head or the tail, thereby removing a lot of headache in writing conditional checks to dealing with null pointers. Be sure to remember to remove them at the end of the operation.

Sometimes linked lists problem can be solved without additional storage. Try to borrow ideas from reverse a linked list problem shown as the first LeetCode online exercise.

For deletion in linked lists, you can either modify the node values or change the node pointers. You might need to keep a reference to the previous element. For partitioning linked lists, create two separate linked lists and join them back together.

Linked lists problems share similarity with array problems, think about how you would do it for an array and try to apply it to a linked list. Two pointer approaches are also common for linked lists. For example:

- Getting the kth from last node - Have two pointers, where one is k nodes ahead of the other. When the node ahead reaches the end, the other node is k nodes behind.
- Detecting cycles - Have two pointers, where one pointer increments twice as much as the other, if the two pointers meet, means that there is a cycle.
- Getting the middle node - Have two pointers, where one pointer increments twice as much as the other. When the faster node reaches the end of the list, the slower node will be at the middle.

Be familiar with the following routines because many linked list questions make use of one or more of these routines in the solution:

- Counting the number of nodes in the linked list.
- Reversing a linked list in-place.
- Finding the middle node of the linked list using fast/slow pointers.
- Merging two lists together.

Corner Cases

- Single node.
- Two nodes.
- Linked list has cycle. Clarify with the interviewer whether there can be a cycle in the list. Usually the answer is no.

Practice Linked List Online

- Reverse a Linked List
- Detect Cycle in a Linked List
- Merge Two Sorted Lists
- Merge K Sorted Lists
- Remove Nth Node From End Of List
- Reorder List

Typical Linked List Interview Questions

1. Write a SortedMerge() function that takes two lists, each of which is sorted in increasing order, and merges the two together into one list which is in increasing order. (Solution)
2. Implement an LRU cache with O(1) runtime for all its operations. (Solution)
3. Given a singly linked list (a list which can only be traversed in one direction), find the item that is located at k items from the end. So if the list is a, b, c, d and k is 2 then the answer is c. The solution should not search the list twice. (Solution)
4. How can you tell if a Linked List is a Palindrome? (Solution)

Tree

A tree is an undirected and connected acyclic graph.

Recursion is a common approach for trees. When you notice that the subtree problem can be used to solve the entire problem, try using recursion. When using recursion, always remember to check for the base case, usually where the node is null.

Recursion is covered as separate topic later in this chapter.

When you are asked to traverse a tree by level, use breadth-first search. Sometimes it is possible that your recursive function needs to return two values. If the question involves summation of nodes along the way, be sure to check whether nodes can be negative.

You should be very familiar with writing pre-order, in-order, and post-order traversal recursively. As an extension, challenge yourself by writing them iteratively. Sometimes interviewers ask candidates for the iterative approach, especially if the candidate finishes writing the recursive approach too quickly.

Corner Cases

- Empty tree.
- Single node.
- Two nodes.
- Very skewed tree (like a linked list).

Binary Tree

In-order traversal of a binary tree is insufficient to uniquely serialize a tree. Pre-order or post-order traversal is also required.

Binary Search Tree (BST)

In-order traversal of a BST will give you all elements in order. Be very familiar with the properties of a BST and validating that a binary tree is a BST. This comes up more often than expected.

When a question involves a BST, the interviewer is usually looking for a solution which runs faster than $O(n)$.

Practice Tree Online

- Maximum Depth of Binary Tree
- Same Tree
- Invert/Flip Binary Tree
- Binary Tree Maximum Path Sum
- Binary Tree Level Order Traversal
- Serialize and Deserialize Binary Tree
- Subtree of Another Tree
- Construct Binary Tree from Preorder and Inorder Traversal
- Validate Binary Search Tree
- Kth Smallest Element in a BST
- Lowest Common Ancestor of BST

Read Further Tree Study Online

- Leaf It Up To Binary Trees

Typical Tree Interview Questions

1. Find the height of a binary tree. (Solution)
2. Find the deepest left leaf of a binary tree. (Solution)
3. Given the roots of a tree. print out all of its root-to-leaf paths one per line. (Solution)
4. Given a binary tree, print level order traversal in a way that nodes of all levels are printed in separate lines. (Solution)
5. Determine if a binary tree is "complete" (i.e, if all leaf nodes were either at the maximum depth or max depth-1, and were 'pressed' along the left side of the tree). (Solution)
6. Determine if a binary tree is a BST. (Solution)
7. Given a binary tree, serialize it into a string. Then deserialize it. (Solution)
8. Given a node, find the next element in a BST. (Solution)
9. Pretty print a JSON object. (Solution)

10. Convert a binary tree to a doubly circular linked list. (Solution)
11. Find the second largest number in a binary tree. (Solution)
12. Convert a tree to a linked list. (Solution)
13. Find the Deepest node in a Binary tree.(Solution

Trie

Tries are special trees (prefix trees) that make searching and storing strings more efficient. Tries have many practical applications, such as conducting searches and providing autocomplete. It is helpful to know these common applications so that you can easily identify when a problem can be efficiently solved using a trie.

Sometimes preprocessing a dictionary of words (given in a list) into a trie, will improve the efficiency of searching for a word of length k, among n words. Searching becomes $O(k)$ instead of $O(n)$.

Be familiar with implementing, from scratch, a Trie class and its add, remove and search methods.

Practice Trie Online

- Implement Trie (Prefix Tree)
- Add and Search Word
- Word Search II

Read Further Trie Study Online

- Trying to Understand Tries
- Implement Trie (Prefix Tree)

Heap

If you see a top or lowest k being mentioned in the question, it is usually a signal that a heap can be used to solve the problem, such as in Top K Frequent Elements.

If you require the top k elements use a Min Heap of size k. Iterate through each element, pushing it into the heap. Whenever the heap size exceeds k, remove the minimum element, that will guarantee that you have the k largest elements.

Practice Heap Online

- Merge K Sorted Lists
- Top K Frequent Elements
- Find Median from Data Stream

Read Further Heap Study Online

- Learning to Love Heaps

Typical Heap Interview Questions

1. Merge K sorted lists together into a single list. (Solution)
2. Given a stream of integers, write an efficient function that returns the median value of the integers. (Solution)

Recursion & Dynamic Programming

Recursion

Recursion is useful for permutation, because it generates all combinations and tree-based questions. You should know how to generate all permutations of a sequence as well as how to handle duplicates.

Remember to always define a base case so that your recursion will end.

Recursion implicitly uses a stack. Hence all recursive approaches can be rewritten iteratively using a stack. Beware of cases where the recursion level goes too deep and causes a stack overflow (for example, the default limit in Python is 1000). You may get bonus points for pointing this out to the interviewer. Recursion will never be O(1) space complexity because a stack is involved, unless there is tail-call optimization (TCO). Beware that TCO is only supported by some programming languages, not all.

Practice Recursion Online

- Longest Univalue Path
- All Possible Full Binary Trees

Typical Recursion Interview Questions

1. Given two number x and y find their product using recursion. (Solution)
2. Given a number, write a function that returns the sum of its digits using recursion. e.g "1234" should return 10. (Solution)

Dynamic Programming

Dynamic Programming (DP) is usually used to solve optimization problems. The only way to get better at DP is to practice. It takes some amount of practice to be able to recognize that a problem can be solved by DP.

Sometimes you do not need to store the whole DP table in memory, the last two values or the last two rows of the matrix will suffice.

Practice Dynamic Programming Online

- Climbing Stairs
- Coin Change
- Longest Increasing Subsequence
- Word Break Problem
- Combination Sum
- House Robber and House Robber II
- Decode Ways
- Unique Paths
- Jump Game

Read Further Dynamic Programming Study Online

- Demystifying Dynamic Programming
- Dynamic Programming – 7 Steps to Solve any DP Interview Problem

Typical Dynamic Programming Interview questions

1. There are N stations on route of a train. The train goes from station 0 to N-1. The ticket cost for all pair of stations (i, j) is given where j is greater than i. Find the minimum cost to reach the destination. (Solution)

2. Given N friends, each one can remain single or can be paired up with some other friend. Each friend can be paired only once. Find out the total number of ways in which friends can remain single or can be paired up. (Solution)

Chapter 3 - Databases

Frequently asked DBMS, SQL, noSQL Interview Questions and answers. Record, Table, Transactions, Locks, Normalization, Foreign Key, Primary Key, Constraints, SQL Commands, Pattern Matching, SQL Joins, Views, Stored procedure, but also NoSQL. This chapter covers basic and more advanced database questions.

General

What is DBMS?

The database management system is a collection of programs that enables user to store, retrieve, update and delete information from a database

What is RDBMS?

Relational Database Management system (RDBMS). It is a database management system (DBMS) that is based on the relational model. Data from relational database can be accessed or reassembled in many different ways without having to reorganize the database tables. Data from relational database can be accessed using an API, Structured Query Language (SQL).

What is SQL?

Structured Query Language(SQL) is a language designed specifically for communicating with databases. SQL is an ANSI (American National Standards Institute) standard.

What is DDL?

DDL stands for Data Definition Language and is used to define the structure that holds the data. For example, Create, Alter, Drop and Truncate table.

What is DML?

DML stands for Data Manipulation Language and is used for manipulation of the data itself. Typical operations are Insert, Delete, Update and retrieving the data from the table. The Select statement is considered as a limited version of the DML, since it can't change the data in the database. But it can perform operations on data retrieved from the DBMS, before the results are returned to the calling function.

What is DCL?

DCL stands for Data Control Language and is used to control the visibility of data like granting database access and set privileges to create tables, etc. Example - Grant, Revoke access permission to the user to access data in the database.

What are the advantages of SQL?

SQL is not a proprietary language used by specific database vendors. Almost every major DBMS supports SQL, so learning this one language will enable programmers to interact with any database like ORACLE, MySQL etc.

SQL is easy to learn. The statements are all made of descriptive keywords.

SQL allow performing very complex and sophisticated database operations.

What is a field in a database?

A field is an area within a record reserved for a specific piece of data.

Examples: Employee Name, Employee ID, etc.

What is a Record in a database?

A record, or row, is the collection of values / fields of a specific entity: i.e. an Employee, Salary etc.

What is a Table in a database?

A table is a collection of records of a specific type. For example, employee table, salary table etc.

Transactions

What is a database transaction?

Database transaction takes a set of database records from one consistent state to another. At the end of the transaction the system must be in the prior state if the transaction fails or the status of the system should reflect the successful completion if the transaction goes through.

What are properties of a transaction?

Expect this SQL Interview Questions as a part of any interview involving databases, irrespective of your experience. Properties of the transaction can be summarized as the ACID properties belows.

Atomicity

A transaction consists of many steps. When all the steps in a transaction get completed, it will get reflected in DB or if any step fails, all the transactions are rolled back.

Consistency

Consistency, states that data cannot be written that would violate the database's own rules for valid data. If a certain transaction occurs that attempts to introduce inconsistent data, the entire transaction is rolled back and an error returned.

A simple rule of consistency may state that the Gender column of a database may only have the values 'Male', 'Female' or 'Unknown'. If a user attempts to enter something else, say 'Hermaphrodite' then a database consistency rule kicks in and disallows the entry of such a value.

Isolation

Every transaction should operate as if it is the only transaction in the system. Transaction isolation is an important part of any transactional system. It deals with consistency and completeness of data retrieved by queries unaffecting a user data by other user actions. A database acquires locks on data to maintain a high level of isolation.

Durability

Once a transaction has completed successfully, the updated rows/records must be available for all other transactions on a permanent basis. Durability guarantees that transactions that have committed will survive permanently. For example, if a flight booking reports that a seat has successfully been booked, then the seat will remain booked even if the system is restarted, or crashes.

Keys and Constraints

What is a primary key?

A primary key is a column whose values uniquely identify every row in a table. Primary key values can never be reused. If a row is deleted from the table, its primary key may not be assigned to any new rows in the future. To define a field as primary key, the following conditions must be met:

- No two rows can have the same primary key value.
- Every row must have a primary key value.
- The primary key field cannot be null.
- Value in a primary key column can never be modified or updated, if any foreign key refers to that primary key.

What is a Composite Key?

A Composite key is a type of key, which represents a set of columns whose values uniquely identify every row in a table. For example - if "Employee_ID" and "Employee Name" in a table is combined to uniquely identify a row its called a Composite key.

What is a Composite Primary Key?

A Composite primary key is a set of columns whose values uniquely identify every row in a table where a table having a composite primary key will be indexed based on the columns specified in the primary key. This key will be referred in Foreign Key tables. For example - if the combined effect of columns, "Employee_ID" and "Employee Name" in a table is required to uniquely identify a row, its called a Composite Primary Key. In this case, both the columns will be represented as primary key.

What is a Foreign Key?

When a table's primary key field is added to a related "many" table in order to create the common field which relates the two tables, it is called a foreign key in those other tables. For example, the salary of an employee is stored in salary table. The relation is established via foreign key column "Employee_ID_Ref" which refers "Employee_ID" field in the Employee table.

Insert, Update and Delete

Define the SQL Insert Statement?

SQL INSERT statement is used to add rows to a table. The SQL query starts with the INSERT INTO statement followed by the table name and values command, followed by the values that need to be inserted into the table.

Example of insert statement:

```
INSERT INTO table_name
    (column1, column2, column3, ...)
VALUES
    (value1, value2, value3, ...);
```

The insert can be used in several ways:

- To insert a single complete row.
- To insert a single partial row.

Define SQL Update Statement?

SQL Update is used to update data in a row or set of rows specified in the filter condition. The basic format of an SQL UPDATE statement is, UPDATE command followed by the table name to be updated and SET command followed by column names and their new values followed by filter condition that determines which rows should be updated.

Example of update statement:

```
UPDATE table_name
SET column1 = value1,
    column2 = value2,
    ...
WHERE condition;
```

Define SQL Delete Statement?

SQL Delete is used to delete a row or set of rows specified in the filter condition. The basic format of an SQL DELETE statement is, DELETE FROM command followed by the table name followed by filter condition that determines which rows should be deleted.

Example of delete statement:

```
DELETE FROM table_name
WHERE condition;
```

How are wild cards used in SQL statements?

SQL Like operator is used for pattern matching. The LIKE command takes more time to process. So before using it as an operator, consider suggestions given below on when and where to use wild card search.

- Do not overuse wild cards. If another search operator will do, use it instead.
- When you do use wild cards, try not to use them at the beginning of the search pattern, unless absolutely necessary. Search patterns that begin with wild cards are the slowest to process.
- Pay careful attention to the placement of the wild card symbols. If they are misplaced, the query might

not return the data you intended.

Joins, Views and Clauses

Define Join and explain different types of joins?

Frequently asked SQL interview questions are on Joins. In order to avoid data duplication, data is stored in related tables. One of the type of JOIN command is used to fetch data from related tables. Joining return rows when there is at least one match in both tables. Commonly used types of joins are covered below.

Right Join Return all rows from the right table, even if there are no matches in the left table.

Left Join Return all rows from the left table, even if there are no matches in the right table.

Inner Join Return rows when there is a match on both tables.

What is Self-Join?

Self-join is when a query joins a table to itself. Aliases should be used for the same table comparison.

What is Cross Join?

Cross Join will return all records where each row from the first table is combined with each row from the second table.

What is the difference between the WHERE clause and the HAVING clause?

WHERE and HAVING both filters out records based on one or more conditions. The difference is, WHERE clause can only be applied on a static non-aggregated column whereas we will need to use HAVING for aggregated columns.

What is a View?

Views are virtual tables. Unlike tables that contain data, views rather contain queries that dynamically retrieve data when used.

What are the advantages and disadvantages using Views?

Advantages

- Views don't store data in a physical location.
- The view can be used to hide some of the columns from the table.
- Views can provide Access Restriction, since data insertion, update and deletion is not possible with the view.

Disadvantages

- When a table is dropped or altered, associated views become irrelevant or need updated as well.
- Complexity where performance suffers because views may be based upon multiple tables. In these cases, queries based upon such views will experience increases in execution time because the database's query processor has to translate these queries in order to query the actual tables of the database from which the columns of the view are derived.

What is a Stored Procedure?

A stored procedure is a function which contains a collection of SQL Queries. The procedure can take inputs, process them and send back output.

What are the advantages of a Stored Procedure?

Stored Procedures are precomplied and stored in the database. This enables the database to execute the queries faster. Since many queries can be included in a stored procedure, round trip time to execute multiple queries from source code to database and back is avoided.

Also, multiple applications can invoke the stored procedure, this can avoid SQL duplication and maintenance across multiple separate consuming applications.

NoSQL

If you are looking for a full stack job, chances are NoSQL knowledge will be very nice to have. You need to prepare for NoSQL Interview Questions. Although every interview is different, the following should give you the necessary to demonstrate understanding of modern database technologies.

What is NoSQL?

NoSQL encompasses a wide variety of different database technologies that were developed in response to a rise in the volume of data stored about users, objects, and products. The frequency at which such large data is accessed impacts performance hence processing have been revisited to suit big data needs. Relational databases were simply not designed to cope with the scale and agility challenges that face modern applications, nor were they built to take advantage of the cheap storage and processing power available today.

What are common features offered by NoSQL Databases?

1. **Flexibility** - NoSQL offers flexibility to store structured, semi-structured or unstructured data.
2. **Dynamic Schemas** - Schema definition is not required, this solves the problem to modify the schema where a table is already present with huge datasets and new columns need to be added to the same table.
3. **Sharding** - Sharding means partitioning data into smaller databases to have faster access to data. This feature is present in most NoSQL databases which allows fetching data from servers in faster time.
4. **Generic** - Can be customized by the user as per the need.
5. **Scaling** - Scales out horizontally, thus cheaper to manage.

Differences with Relational DB?

RDBMS over NoSQL

- Better for relational data that is structured and organized.
- Organize data through normalization
- Use Structured query language(SQL) which is easy to learn
- Maintains Data Integrity
- Data and its relationships are stored in separate tables
- ACID compliance, i.e. either all the transactions are committed or none.
- Scale up / Vertical Scaling

NoSQL over RDBMS

- Better or easier for unstructured and unpredictable data
- No predefined schema
- Usually Cheaper to manage
- Higher performance, availability, and scalability for Big Data
- Scale-out / Horizontal Scaling

What are the different types of NoSQL databases?

Four different types of NoSQL databases

1. **Key-value stores** - The simplest, where every item in the database is stored as an attribute name (or key) together with its value. Riak, Voldemort, and Redis are the most well-known in this category.
2. **Wide-column stores** - It stores the data together as columns instead of rows and is optimized for queries over large datasets. The most popular are Cassandra and HBase.
3. **Document databases** - It pairs each key with a complex data structure known as a document. Documents can contain many different key-value pairs, or key-array pairs, or even nested documents. MongoDB is the most popular of these databases.
4. **Graph databases** - They are used to store information about networks, such as social connections. Examples are Neo4J and HyperGraphDB.

Do you know what is BASE?

The CAP theorem states that distributed systems cannot achieve all three properties at the same time:

- Consistency

- Availability
- Partition tolerance

The BASE (Basically Available Soft state Eventual consistency) system gives up on consistency while maintaining the other two. The BASE system works well despite physical network partitions and always allow a client with reading and write availability.

Chapter 4 - Networking

In the software development industry, there can hardly be anyone who has never coded applications connected to a form of network. In the past, when software developers entered the interview room, they could be assured that the questions would focus purely on evaluating programming skills. Nowadays it is important to have the networking basics covered.

Interviewers like to measure the developer's ability to grasps networking terms and how the internet works.

General

What is a Network?

A network is a set of devices connected to each other using a physical transmission medium. Example: A Computer Network is a group of computers connected with each other to communicate and share information and resources like hardware, data, and software across each other. In a network, nodes are used to connect two or more networks.

What is Network Topology?

Network Topology is a physical layout of the computer network. It defines how the computers, devices, cables and other assets are connected to each other.

What is a Router?

A router is a network device which connects two or more network segments. The router is used to transfer information from source to destination. Routers send the information in terms of data packets and when these data packets are forwarded from one router to another router then the router reads the network address in the packets and identifies the destination network.

What are the layers in OSI Reference Models?

Given below are the seven layers of OSI Reference Models:

1. **Physical Layer** (Layer 1): Physical Layer converts data bits into electrical impulse or radio signals. E.g. Ethernet.
2. **Data Link Layer** (Layer 2): At Data Link layer, data packets are encoded and decoded into bits and it provides a node to node data transfer. Data Link Layer also detects the errors occurred at Layer 1.
3. **Network Layer** (Layer 3): Network Layer transfers variable length data sequence from one node to another node in the same network. This variable length data sequence is also known as "Datagrams".
4. **Transport Layer** (Layer 4): It transfers data between nodes and also provides acknowledgment of successful data transmission. It keeps track of transmission and sends the segments again if the transmission fails
5. **Session Layer** (Layer 5): Session Layer manages and controls the connections between computers. It establishes, coordinates, exchange and terminates the connections between local and the remote applications.
6. **Presentation Layer** (Layer 6): It is also called as "Syntax Layer". Layer 6 transforms the data into the form in which the application layer accepts.
7. **Application Layer** (Layer 7): This is the last layer of OSI Reference Model and is the one which is close to the end user. Both end-user and application layer interacts with the software application. This layer provides services for email, file transfer etc.

How can a network be certified as an effective network? What are the factors affecting them?

A network can be certified as an effective network based on below-mentioned points:

- **Performance**: A network's performance is based on its transmitted time and response time. The factors affecting the performance of a network are hardware, software, transmission medium types and the number of users using the network.
- **Reliability**: Reliability is nothing but measuring the probability of failures occurred in a network and the time taken by it to recover from it. The factors affecting the same are the frequency of failure and recovery time from failure.
- **Security**: Protecting the data from malware and unauthorized users. The factors affecting the security are malware and users who do not have permission to access the network.

Protocols

Explain the TCP/IP Model

It stands for Transmission Control Protocol and Internet Protocol and is the most widely used and available protocol. TCP/IP specifies how data should be packaged, transmitted and routed in their end to end data communication.

It consists of 4 layers:

1. **Application Layer**: This is the top layer in TCP/IP model. It includes processes which use Transport Layer Protocol to transmit the data to their destination. There are different Application Layer

Protocols such as HTTP, FTP, SMTP, SNMP protocols etc.

2. **Transport Layer**: It receives the data from the Application Layer which is above Transport Layer. It acts as a backbone between the host's system connected with each other and it mainly concerns the transmission of data. TCP and UDP are mainly used as a Transport Layer protocols.

3. **Network or Internet Layer**: This layer sends the packets across the network. Packets mainly contain source & destination IP addresses and actual data to be transmitted.

4. **Network Interface Layer**: It is the lowest layer of TCP/IP model. It transfers the packets between different hosts. It includes encapsulation of IP packets into frames, mapping IP addresses to physical hardware devices etc.

What is HTTP and what port does it use?

HTTP is HyperText Transfer Protocol and it is responsible for web content. Many web pages are using HTTP to transmit the web content and allow the display and navigation of HyperText.

It is the primary protocol and the default port used is TCP port 80.

What is HTTPs and what port does it use?

HTTPS is a Secure HTTP. HTTPS is used for encrypted and secure communication over a computer network to prevent man in the middle attack and sniffing.

In a bi-directional communication, HTTPS protocol encrypts the communication so that tampering of the data gets avoided. With the help of a SSL certificate, it verifies if the requested server connection is a valid connection or not. HTTPS uses TCP with port 443.

What is an IP Address?

IP address stands for Internet Protocol Address. It is a unique string of numbers used to specify the location of a computer or other device in a network using TCP/IP. It is represented by a series of four decimal numbers, separated by dots. Example: 192.168.101.4

How can you identify the IP of a workstation?

Using the command line:

```
$ifconfig (Linux)
```

or

```
$ipconfig (Windows)
```

What is the difference between IPv4 and IPv6?

IPv4 is a 32-bit address scheme which allows a total 2^{32} number of addresses.

IPv6 is 4 times larger than IPv4. It is 128 bit address scheme and allows total 2^{128} number of addresses.

Explain DNS?

DNS stands for Domain Naming Server. DNS acts as a translator between domain names and IP address. As humans remember names, the computer understands only numbers. Generally, we assign names to websites and computers like google.com wikipedia.com etc. When we type such names the DNS translates it into numbers and execute the requests.

- Translating the hostname into IP address is called a Forward lookup.
- Translating the IP address to hostname is called a Reverse lookup.

Chapter 5 - Security

Some background on Cyber Security is always desirable when applying for a technical job, all software developers are now expected to have acquired some knowledge on the subject.

Encryption

What is Symmetrical Encryption?

- Symmetrical encryption is a type of encryption where the same key is used to encrypt plaintext messages and to decrypt ciphertext.
- Symmetrical encryption is usually much less computationally expensive as compared to asymmetric encryption.
- Often called "shared secret" encryption, or "secret key" encryption.
- To use a symmetric encryption scheme, the sender and receiver must securely share a key in advance. This sharing can be done via asymmetric encryption.

What is Asymmetric Encryption?

- A pair of keys are required: a **private key** and a **public key**. Public keys can be shared with anyone while private keys should be kept secret and known only to the owner.
- A private key can be used to decrypt a message encrypted by the corresponding public key. A successful decryption verifies that the holder possesses the private key.
- Also known as public-key cryptography.

What is Public Key Infrastructure?

A public key infrastructure (PKI) is a system for the creation, storage, and distribution of digital certificates which are used to verify that a particular public key belongs to a certain entity. The PKI creates digital certificates which map public keys to entities, securely stores these certificates in a central repository and revokes them if needed.

References

- https://www.wikiwand.com/en/Public_key_infrastructure

What is the difference between encryption and hashing?

- Encryption is reversible whereas hashing is irreversible. Hashing can be cracked using rainbow tables and collision attacks but is not reversible.
- Encryption is reversible, assuming one has the key, it ensures confidentiality whereas hashing ensures Integrity.

SSH

An SSH session consists of two stages, **Negotiating Encryption** and **User Authentication**.

How does SSH Negotiating Encryption work?

The goal of this stage is for the client and server to agree upon and establish encryption to protect future communication, by generating an identical session key. One possible algorithm to generate the session key is the Diffie–Hellman key exchange scheme. Each party generates a public/private key pair and exchanges the public key.

After obtaining an authentic copy of each other's public keys, each party can compute a shared secret offline.

The basis of this procedure for classic Diffie-Hellman is:

1. Both parties agree on a large prime number, which will serve as a seed value.
2. Both parties agree on an encryption generator (typically AES), which will be used to manipulate the values in a predefined way.
3. Independently, each party comes up with another prime number which is kept secret from the other party. This number is used as the private key for this interaction (different than the private SSH key used for authentication).
4. The generated private key, the encryption generator, and the shared prime number are used to generate a public key that is derived from the private key, but which can be shared with the other party.
5. Both participants then exchange their generated public keys.
6. The receiving entity uses their own private key, the other party's public key, and the original shared prime number to compute a shared secret key.
7. Although this is independently computed by each party, using opposite private and public keys, it will result in the same shared secret key.
8. The shared secret is then used to encrypt all communication that follows.

The purpose of the shared secret key is to wrap all further communication in an encrypted tunnel that cannot be deciphered by outsiders.

How does SSH User Authentication work?

The goal of this stage is to authenticate the user and discover whether access to the server should be granted. There are two approaches for authenticating, either by using passwords, or SSH key pairs.

For password authentication, the server simply prompts the client for the password of the account they are attempting to login with. The password is sent through the negotiated encryption, so it is secure from outside parties.

Authentication using SSH key pairs begins after the symmetric encryption has been established as described in the last section. The procedure happens like this:

1. The client begins by sending an ID for the key pair it would like to authenticate with the server.
2. The server check's the authorized_keys file of the account that the client is attempting to log into for the key ID.
3. If a public key with matching ID is found in the file, the server generates a random number and uses the public key to encrypt the number.
4. The server sends the client this encrypted message.
5. If the client actually has the associated private key, it will be able to decrypt the message using that key, revealing the original number.
6. The client combines the decrypted number with the shared session key that is being used to encrypt the communication, and calculates the SHA256 hash of this value.
7. The client then sends this SHA256 hash back to the server as an answer to the encrypted number message.
8. The server uses the same shared session key and the original number that it sent to the client to calculate the SHA256 value on its own. It compares its own

calculation to the one that the client sent back. If these two values match, it proves that the client was in possession of the private key and the client is authenticated.

References

- https://www.digitalocean.com/community/tutorials/understanding-the-ssh-encryption-and-connection-process

What is SHA-256?

SHA-256 stands for Secure Hash Algorithm – 256 bit and is a type of hash function commonly to hash collision proof values. A hash function is a type of mathematical function which turns data into a fingerprint of that data called a hash.

What about MD5?

MD5 is another hashing algorithm, which is now known to be vulnerable to collision attack.

Common Web Application Vulnerabilities

What is XSS? How would you mitigate it?

XSS stands for Cross Site Scripting and is a commonly found JavaScript vulnerability in web applications. The easiest way to explain it is with a case when a user enters a script in the client side input fields and that input gets processed without getting validated. This leads to untrusted code getting saved or reflected, and then executed on the client side.

Countermeasures of XSS are input validation and/or output escaping.

What is the difference between stored XSS and reflected XSS?

In case of Stored XSS, the script is stored, generally on a backend, it is fetched by the webpage and executed on the client browser. Reflected XSS, on the other hand, require the user to send a request first. The request will start running on the browser of the victim's computer and then will reflect the results back from the website or the browser to the user who has sent the request.

What is CSRF?

Cross Site Request Forgery is a web application vulnerability in which the server does not check whether the request came from a trusted client or not. The request usually gets processed on behalf of a user without its consent, usually coupled with a XSS vulnerability to perform the exploit.

How can you defend a web application against CSRF attacks?

Require every request to include a random token only present on the trusted scope of the web client.

What is SQL injection?

SQL Injection is a very common application layer attack techniques that takes advantage of improper coding of a web application that would allows hacker to inject SQL commands into say a login form to allow them to gain access to the data held within the database.

How to mitigate the risk SQL injections?

The most effective measure against SQL Injection is to use prepared statements throughout the application where the code is building SQL statements. Prepared statements ensure escaping of input values so that no statement execution can be altered by the end user.

Chapter 6 - HTML5 & CSS

If you're on your way to an interview for any role mentioning front end development or web apps, you can be pretty confident that they'll quiz you on HTML5 and CSS. If you're still new to the standards of the web, this can be pretty daunting. There's a lot of history and things are changing all the time.

Make sure to practice your front end skills, if you are unfamiliar with front end development, I recommend following through the first few sections of the freecodecamp's curriculum. It is packed with lessons and online exercises.

This chapter covers the most commonly asked HTML5 and CSS interview questions. It will help you demonstrate you grasp the basics, some of the newer tricks, and that you know how to stay up to date - which will go a long way towards improving your chances of securing the coveted job.

HTML5

What does a DOCTYPE do?

DOCTYPE is an abbreviation for **DOCument TYPE**.
A DOCTYPE is always associated to a **DTD** - for **Document Type Definition**.

A DTD defines how documents of a certain type should be structured (i.e. a button can contain a span but not a div), whereas a DOCTYPE declares what DTD a document *supposedly* respects (i.e. this document respects the HTML DTD).

For webpages, the DOCTYPE declaration is required. It is used to tell user agents what version of the HTML specifications your document respects.
Once a user agent has recognized a correct DOCTYPE, it will trigger the **no-quirks mode** matching this DOCTYPE for reading the document.
If a user agent doesn't recognize a correct DOCTYPE, it will trigger the **quirks mode**.

The DOCTYPE declaration for the HTML5 standards is <!DOCTYPE html>.

References

- https://html.spec.whatwg.org/multipage/syntax.html#the-doctype
- https://html.spec.whatwg.org/multipage/xhtml.html
- https://quirks.spec.whatwg.org/

How would you serve a page with content in multiple languages?

The question is a little vague, I will assume that it is asking about the most common case, which is how to serve a page with content available in multiple languages, but the content within the page should be displayed only in one consistent language.

When an HTTP request is made to a server, the requesting user agent usually sends information about language preferences, such as in the Accept-Language header. The server can then use this information to return a version of the document in the appropriate language if such an alternative is available. The returned HTML document should also declare the lang attribute in the <html> tag, such as <html lang="en">...</html>.

In the back end, the HTML markup will contain i18n placeholders and content for the specific language stored in YML or JSON formats. The server then dynamically generates the HTML page with content in that particular language, usually with the help of a back end i18n framework.

Note that front end i18n frameworks also exists, where the content is *rendered* by the browser, usually through JavaScript, in the user language preference.

References

- https://www.w3.org/International/getting-started/language

What kind of things must you be wary of when designing or developing for multilingual sites?

- Use lang attribute in your HTML.
- Directing users to their native language - Allow a user to change his country/language easily without hassle.
- Text in images is not a scalable approach - Placing text in an image is still a popular way to get good-looking, non-system fonts to display on any computer. However, to translate image text, each string of text will need to have it's a separate image created for each language. Anything more than a handful of replacements like this can quickly get out of control.
- Restrictive words/sentence length - Some content can be longer when written in another language. Be wary of layout or overflow issues in the design. It's best to avoid designing where the amount of text would make or break a design. Character counts come into play with things like headlines, labels, and buttons. They are less of an issue with free-flowing text such as body text or comments.
- Be mindful of how colors are perceived - Colors are perceived differently across languages and cultures. The design should use color appropriately.
- Formatting dates and currencies - Calendar dates are sometimes presented in different ways. Eg. "May 31, 2012" in the U.S. vs. "31 May 2012" in parts of Europe.
- Do not concatenate translated strings - Do not do anything like "The date today is " + date. It will break in languages with different word order. Use a template string with parameters substitution for each language instead. For example, look at the following two sentences in English and Chinese respectively: I will travel on {% date %} and {% date %} 我会出发. Note that

the position of the variable is different due to grammar rules of the language.

- Language reading direction - In English, we read from left-to-right, top-to-bottom, in traditional Japanese, text is read up-to-down, right-to-left.

References

- https://www.quora.com/What-kind-of-things-one-should-be-wary-of-when-designing-or-developing-for-multilingual-sites

What are data- attributes good for?

Before JavaScript frameworks became popular, front end developers used data- attributes to store extra data within the DOM itself, without other hacks such as non-standard attributes, extra properties on the DOM. It is intended to store custom data private to the page or application, for which there are no more appropriate attributes or elements.

These days, using data- attributes is not encouraged. One reason is that users can modify the data attribute easily by using inspect element in the browser. The data model is better stored within JavaScript itself and stay updated with the DOM via data binding possibly through a library or a framework.

References

- http://html5doctor.com/html5-custom-data-attributes/
- https://www.w3.org/TR/html5/dom.html#embedding-custom-non-visible-data-with-the-data-*-attributes

Consider HTML5 as an open web platform. What are the building blocks of HTML5?

- **Semantics** - Allowing you to describe more precisely what your content is.
- **Connectivity** - Allowing you to communicate with the server in new and innovative ways.
- **Offline and storage** - Allowing webpages to store data on the client-side locally and operate offline more efficiently.
- **Multimedia** - Making video and audio first-class citizens in the Open Web.
- **2D/3D graphics and effects** - Allowing a much more diverse range of presentation options.
- **Performance and integration** - Providing greater speed optimization and better usage of computer hardware.
- **Device access** - Allowing for the usage of various input and output devices.
- **Styling** - Letting authors write more sophisticated themes.

References

- https://developer.mozilla.org/en-US/docs/Web/Guide/HTML/HTML5

Describe the difference between a cookie, sessionStorage and localStorage.

All the above-mentioned technologies are key-value storage mechanisms on the client side. They are only able to store values as strings.

Cookie

- Max size of 4093 bytes
- Can set expiration date
- Sent on every request

sessionStorage

- Max size of 2.5MBs+ depending on browser
- Stored in browser and not sent with every request
- If you close a tab using sessionStorage, open a new tab, or exit the browser - you'll lose that specific sessionStorage data.

localStorage

- Max size of 2.5MBs+ depending on browser
- Stored in browser and not sent with every request
- Will persist if browser/tabs are closed.

References

- https://developer.mozilla.org/en-US/docs/Web/HTTP/Cookies
- http://tutorial.techaltum.com/local-and-session-storage.html

Describe the difference between <script>, <script async> and <script defer>.

- <script> - HTML parsing is blocked, the script is fetched and executed immediately, HTML parsing resumes after the script is executed.
- <script async> - The script will be fetched in parallel to HTML parsing and executed as soon as it is available (potentially before HTML parsing completes). Use async when the script is independent

of any other scripts on the page, for example, analytics.

- <script defer> - The script will be fetched in parallel to HTML parsing and executed when the page has finished parsing. If there are multiple of them, each deferred script is executed in the order they were encountered in the document. If a script relies on a fully-parsed DOM, the defer attribute will be useful in ensuring that the HTML is fully parsed before executing. There's not much difference in putting a normal <script> at the end of <body>. A deferred script must not contain document.write.

Note: The async and defer attributes are ignored for scripts that have no src attribute.

References

- http://www.growingwiththeweb.com/2014/02/async -vs-defer-attributes.html
- https://stackoverflow.com/questions/10808109/scrip t-tag-async-defer
- https://bitsofco.de/async-vs-defer/

Why is it generally a good idea to position CSS <link>s between <head></head> and JS <script>s just before </body>? Do you know any exceptions?

Placing <link>s in the <head>

Putting <link>s in the head is part of the specification. Besides that, placing at the top allows the page to render progressively which improves the user experience. The problem with putting stylesheets near the bottom of the document is that it prohibits progressive rendering in many browsers, including Internet Explorer. Some browsers block rendering to avoid having to repaint elements of the page if their styles change. The user is stuck viewing a blank white page. It prevents the flash of unstyled contents.

Placing <script>s just before </body>

<script>s block HTML parsing while they are being downloaded and executed. Downloading the scripts at the bottom will allow the HTML to be parsed and displayed to the user first.

An exception for positioning of <script>s at the bottom is when your script contains document.write(), but these days it's not a good practice to use document.write(). Also, placing <script>s at the bottom means that the browser cannot start downloading the scripts until the entire document is parsed. One possible workaround is to put <script> in the <head> and use the defer attribute.

References

- https://developer.yahoo.com/performance/rules.html #css_top

What is progressive rendering?

Progressive rendering is the name given to techniques used to improve the performance of a webpage (in particular, improve perceived load time) to render content for display as quickly as possible.

It used to be much more prevalent in the days before broadband internet but it is still used in modern development as mobile data connections are becoming increasingly popular (and unreliable)!

Examples of such techniques:

- **Lazy loading of images** - Images on the page are not loaded all at once. JavaScript will be used to load an image when the user scrolls into the part of the page that displays the image.
- **Prioritizing visible content (or above-the-fold rendering)** - Include only the minimum CSS/content/scripts necessary for the amount of page that would be rendered in the users browser first to display as quickly as possible, you can then use deferred scripts or listen for the DOMContentLoaded/load event to load in other resources and content.
- **Async HTML fragments** - Flushing parts of the HTML to the browser as the page is constructed on the back end.

References

- https://stackoverflow.com/questions/33651166/what-is-progressive-rendering
- http://www.ebaytechblog.com/2014/12/08/async-fragments-rediscovering-progressive-html-rendering-with-marko/

Why you would use a srcset attribute in an image tag? Explain the process the browser uses when evaluating the content of this attribute.

You would use the srcset attribute when you want to serve different images to users depending on their device display width - serve higher quality images to devices with retina display enhances the user experience while serving lower resolution images to low-end devices increase performance and decrease data wastage (because serving a larger image will not have any visible difference). For example: <img srcset="small.jpg 500w, medium.jpg 1000w, large.jpg 2000w"> tells the browser to display the small, medium or large .jpg graphic depending on the client's resolution. The first value is the image name and the second is the width of the image in pixels. For a device width of 320px, the following calculations are made:

- $500 / 320 = 1.5625$
- $1000 / 320 = 3.125$
- $2000 / 320 = 6.25$

If the client's resolution is 1x, 1.5625 is the closest, and 500w corresponding to small.jpg will be selected by the browser.

If the resolution is retina (2x), the browser will use the closest resolution above the minimum. Meaning it will not choose the 500w (1.5625) because it is greater than 1 and the image might look bad. The browser would then choose the image with a resulting ratio closer to 2 which is 1000w (3.125).

srcsets solve the problem whereby you want to serve smaller image files to narrow screen devices, as they don't need huge images like desktop displays do — and also optionally that you want to serve different resolution images to high density/low-density screens.

References

- https://developer.mozilla.org/en-US/docs/Learn/HTML/Multimedia_and_embedding/Responsive_images

- https://css-tricks.com/responsive-images-youre-just-changing-resolutions-use-srcset/

Have you used different HTML templating languages before?

Yes, Pug (formerly Jade), ERB, Slim, Handlebars, Jinja, Liquid, just to name a few. In my opinion, they are more or less the same and provide similar functionality of escaping content and helpful filters for manipulating the data to be displayed. Most templating engines will also allow you to inject your own filters in the event you need custom processing before display.

CSS

What is CSS selector specificity and how does it work?

The browser determines what styles to show on an element depending on the specificity of CSS rules. We assume that the browser has already determined the rules that match a particular element. Among the matching rules, the specificity, four comma-separate values, a, b, c, d are calculated for each rule based on the following:

1. a is whether inline styles are being used. If the property declaration is an inline style on the element, a is 1, else 0.
2. b is the number of ID selectors.
3. c is the number of classes, attributes and pseudo-classes selectors.
4. d is the number of tags and pseudo-elements selectors.

The resulting specificity is not a score, but a matrix of values that can be compared column by column. When comparing selectors to determine which has the highest specificity, look from left to right, and compare the highest value in each column. So a value in column b will override values in columns c and d, no matter what they might be. As such, specificity of 0,1,0,0 would be greater than one of 0,0,10,10.

In the cases of equal specificity: the latest rule is the one that counts. If you have written the same rule into your stylesheet (regardless of internal or external) twice, then the lower rule in your style sheet is closer to the element to be styled, it is deemed to be more specific and therefore will be applied.

I would write CSS rules with low specificity so that they can be easily overridden if necessary. When writing CSS UI component library code, it is important that they have low specificities so that users of the library can override them without using too complicated CSS rules just for the sake of increasing specificity or resorting to !important.

References

- https://www.smashingmagazine.com/2007/07/css-specificity-things-you-should-know/
- https://www.sitepoint.com/web-foundations/specificity/

What's the difference between "resetting" and "normalizing" CSS? Which would you choose, and why?

- **Resetting** - Resetting is meant to strip all default browser styling on elements. For e.g. margins, paddings, font-sizes of all elements are reset to be the same. You will have to redeclare styling for common typographic elements.
- **Normalizing** - Normalizing preserves useful default styles rather than "unstyling" everything. It also corrects bugs for common browser dependencies.

I would choose resetting when I have a very customized or unconventional site design such that I need to do a lot of my own styling and do not need any default styling to be preserved.

References

- https://stackoverflow.com/questions/6887336/what-is-the-difference-between-normalize-css-and-reset-css

Describe floats and how they work

Float is a CSS positioning property. Floated elements remain a part of the flow of the page, and will affect the positioning of other elements (e.g. text will flow around floated elements), unlike position: absolute elements, which are removed from the flow of the page.

The CSS clear property can be used to be positioned below left/right/both floated elements.

If a parent element contains nothing but floated elements, its height will be collapsed to nothing. It can be fixed by clearing the float after the floated elements in the container but before the close of the container.

The .clearfix hack uses a clever CSS pseudo selector (:after) to clear floats. Rather than setting the overflow on the parent, you apply an additional class clearfix to it. Then apply this CSS:

```
.clearfix:after {
  content: ' ';
  visibility: hidden;
  display: block;
  height: 0;
  clear: both;
}
```

Alternatively, give overflow: auto or overflow: hidden property to the parent element which will establish a new block formatting context inside the children and it will expand to contain its children.

References

- https://css-tricks.com/all-about-floats/

Describe z-index and how stacking context is formed

The z-index property in CSS controls the vertical stacking order of elements that overlap. z-index only affects elements that have a position value which is not static.

Without any z-index value, elements stack in the order that they appear in the DOM (the lowest one down at the same hierarchy level appears on top). Elements with non-static positioning (and their children) will always appear on top of elements with default static positioning, regardless of HTML hierarchy.

A stacking context is an element that contains a set of layers. Within a local stacking context, the z-index values of its children are set relative to that element rather than to the document root. Layers outside of that context — i.e. sibling elements of a local stacking context — can't sit between layers within it. If an element B sits on top of element A, a child element of element A, element C, can never be higher than element B even if element C has a higher z-index than element B.

Each stacking context is self-contained - after the element's contents are stacked, the whole element is considered in the stacking order of the parent stacking context. A handful of CSS properties trigger a new stacking context, such as opacity less than 1, filter that is not none, and transform that is not none.

References

- https://css-tricks.com/almanac/properties/z/z-index/
- https://philipwalton.com/articles/what-no-one-told-you-about-z-index/
- https://developer.mozilla.org/en-US/docs/Web/CSS/CSS_Positioning/Understanding_z_index/The_stacking_context

Describe Block Formatting Context (BFC) and how it works

A Block Formatting Context (BFC) is part of the visual CSS rendering of a web page in which block boxes are laid out. Floats, absolutely positioned elements, inline-blocks, table-cells, table-captions, and elements with overflow other than visible (except when that value has been propagated to the viewport) establish new block formatting contexts.

A BFC is an HTML box that satisfies at least one of the following conditions:

- The value of float is not none.
- The value of position is neither static nor relative.
- The value of display is table-cell, table-caption, inline-block, flex, or inline-flex.
- The value of overflow is not visible.

In a BFC, each box's left outer edge touches the left edge of the containing block (for right-to-left formatting, right edges touch).

Vertical margins between adjacent block-level boxes in a BFC collapse.

References

- https://developer.mozilla.org/en-US/docs/Web/Guide/CSS/Block_formatting_context
- https://www.sitepoint.com/understanding-block-formatting-contexts-in-css/
- https://www.sitepoint.com/web-foundations/collapsing-margins/).

What are the various clearing techniques and which is appropriate for what context?

- Empty div method - .
- Clearfix method - Refer to the .clearfix class above.
- overflow: auto or overflow: hidden method - Parent will establish a new block formatting context and expand to contains its floated children.

In large projects, I would write a utility .clearfix class and use them in places where I need it. overflow: hidden might clip children if the children is taller than the parent hence is not ideal.

Explain CSS sprites, and how you would implement them on a page or site

CSS sprites combine multiple images into one single larger image. It is a commonly-used technique for icons (Gmail uses it). How to implement it:

1. Use a sprite generator that packs multiple images into one and generate the appropriate CSS for it.
2. Each image would have a corresponding CSS class with background-image, background-position and

background-size properties defined.

3. To use that image, add the corresponding class to your element.

Advantages:

- Reduce the number of HTTP requests for multiple images (only one single request is required per spritesheet). But with HTTP2, loading multiple images is no longer much of an issue.
- Advance downloading of assets that won't be downloaded until needed, such as images that only appear upon :hover pseudo-states. Blinking wouldn't be seen.

References

- https://css-tricks.com/css-sprites/

How would you approach fixing browser-specific styling issues?

- After identifying the issue and the offending browser, use a separate style sheet that only loads when that specific browser is being used. This technique requires server-side rendering though.
- Use libraries like Bootstrap that already handles these styling issues for you.
- Use autoprefixer to automatically add vendor prefixes to your code.
- Use Reset CSS or Normalize.css.

How do you serve your pages for feature-constrained browsers? What techniques/processes do you use?

- Graceful degradation - The practice of building an application for modern browsers while ensuring it remains functional in older browsers.

- Progressive enhancement - The practice of building an application for a base level of user experience, but adding functional enhancements when a browser supports it.
- Use caniuse.com to check for feature support.
- Autoprefixer for automatic vendor prefix insertion.
- Feature detection using Modernizr.
- Use CSS Feature queries @support

What are the different ways to visually hide content (and make it available only for screen readers)?

These techniques are related to accessibility (a11y).

- visibility: hidden. However, the element is still in the flow of the page, and still takes up space.
- width: 0; height: 0. Make the element not take up any space on the screen at all, resulting in not showing it.
- position: absolute; left: -99999px. Position it outside of the screen.
- text-indent: -9999px. This only works on text within the block elements.
- Metadata. For example by using Schema.org, RDF, and JSON-LD.
- WAI-ARIA. A W3C technical specification that specifies how to increase the accessibility of web pages.

Even if WAI-ARIA is the ideal solution, I would go with the absolute positioning approach, as it has the least caveats, works for most elements and it's an easy technique.

References

- https://www.w3.org/TR/wai-aria-1.1/

- https://developer.mozilla.org/en-US/docs/Web/Accessibility/ARIA
- http://a11yproject.com/

Have you ever used a grid system, and if so, which do you prefer?

I like the float-based grid system because it still has the most browser support among the alternative existing systems (flex, grid). It has been used in Bootstrap for years and has been proven to work.

Have you used or implemented media queries or mobile-specific layouts/CSS?

Yes. An example would be transforming a stacked pill navigation into a fixed-bottom tab navigation beyond a certain breakpoint.

Are you familiar with styling SVG?

Yes, there are several ways to color shapes (including specifying attributes on the object) using inline CSS, an embedded CSS section, or an external CSS file. Most SVG you'll find around the web use inline CSS, but there are advantages and disadvantages associated with each type.

Basic coloring can be done by setting two attributes on the node: fill and stroke. fill sets the color inside the object and stroke sets the color of the line drawn around the object. You can use the same CSS color naming schemes that you use in HTML, whether that's color names (that is red), RGB values (that is rgb(255,0,0)), Hex values, RGBA values, etc.

```
<rect x="10" y="10" width="100"
  height="100" stroke="blue"
  fill="purple" fill-opacity="0.5"
  stroke-opacity="0.8"/>
```

References

- https://developer.mozilla.org/en-US/docs/Web/SVG/Tutorial/Fills_and_Strokes

Can you give an example of an @media property other than screen?

Yes, there are four types of @media properties (including *screen*):

- all - for all media type devices
- print - for printers
- speech - for screen readers that "reads" the page out loud
- screen - for computer screens, tablets, smart-phones etc.

Here is an example of print media type's usage:

```
@media print {
  body {
    color: black;
  }
}
```

References

- https://developer.mozilla.org/en-US/docs/Web/CSS/@media#Syntax

What are some of the "gotchas" for writing efficient CSS?

Firstly, understand that browsers match selectors from rightmost (key selector) to left. Browsers filter out elements in the DOM according to the key selector and traverse up its parent elements to determine matches. The shorter the length of the selector chain, the faster the browser can determine if that element matches the selector. Hence avoid key selectors that are tag and universal selectors. They match a large number of elements and browsers will have to do more work in determining if the parents do match.

BEM (Block Element Modifier) methodology recommends that everything has a single class, and, where you need hierarchy, that gets baked into the name of the class as well, this naturally makes the selector efficient and easy to override.

Be aware of which CSS properties trigger reflow, repaint, and compositing. Avoid writing styles that change the layout (trigger reflow) where possible.

References

- https://developers.google.com/web/fundamentals/performance/rendering/
- https://csstriggers.com/

What are the advantages/disadvantages of using CSS preprocessors?

Advantages:

- CSS is made more maintainable.
- Easy to write nested selectors.
- Variables for consistent theming. Can share theme files across different projects.
- Mixins to generate repeated CSS.
- Splitting your code into multiple files. CSS files can be split up too but doing so will require an HTTP request to download each CSS file.

Disadvantages:

- Requires tools for preprocessing. Re-compilation time can be slow.

Describe what you like and dislike about the CSS preprocessors you have used

Likes:

- Mostly the advantages mentioned above.
- Less is written in JavaScript.

Dislikes:

- I use Sass via node-sass, which is a binding for LibSass written in C++. I have to frequently recompile it when switching between node versions.
- In Less, variable names are prefixed with @, which can be confused with native CSS keywords like @media, @import and @font-face rule.

How would you implement a web design comp that uses non-standard fonts?

Use @font-face and define font-family for different font-weights.

Explain how a browser determines what elements match a CSS selector.

This part is related to the above about writing efficient CSS. Browsers match selectors from rightmost (key selector) to left. Browsers filter out elements in the DOM according to the key selector and traverse up its parent elements to determine matches. The shorter the length of the selector chain, the faster the browser can determine if that element matches the selector.

For example with this selector p span, browsers firstly find all the <span> elements and traverse up its parent all the way up to the root to find the <p> element. For a particular <span>, as soon as it finds a <p>, it knows that the <span> matches and can stop its matching.

References

- https://stackoverflow.com/questions/5797014/why-do-browsers-match-css-selectors-from-right-to-left

Describe pseudo-elements and discuss what they are used for

A CSS pseudo-element is a keyword added to a selector that lets you style a specific part of the selected element(s). They can be used for decoration (:first-line, :first-letter) or adding elements to the markup (combined with content: ...) without having to modify the markup (:before, :after).

- :first-line and :first-letter can be used to decorate text.
- Used in the .clearfix hack as shown above to add a zero-space element with clear: both.
- Triangular arrows in tooltips use :before and :after. Encourages separation of concerns because the

triangle is considered part of styling and not really the DOM. It's not really possible to draw a triangle with just CSS styles without using an additional HTML element.

References

* https://css-tricks.com/almanac/selectors/a/after-and-before/

Explain your understanding of the box model and how you would tell the browser in CSS to render your layout in different box models

The CSS box model describes the rectangular boxes that are generated for elements in the document tree and laid out according to the visual formatting model. Each box has a content area (e.g. text, an image, etc.) and optional surrounding padding, border, and margin areas.

The CSS box model is responsible for calculating:

* How much space a block element takes up.
* Whether or not borders and/or margins overlap, or collapse.
* A box's dimensions.

The box model has the following rules:

* The dimensions of a block element are calculated by width, height, padding, borders, and margins.
* If no height is specified, a block element will be as high as the content it contains, plus padding (unless there are floats, for which see below).
* If no width is specified, a non-floated block element will expand to fit the width of its parent minus

padding.
- The height of an element is calculated by the content's height.
- The width of an element is calculated by the content's width.
- By default, paddings and borders are not part of the width and height of an element.

References

- https://www.smashingmagazine.com/2010/06/the-principles-of-cross-browser-css-coding/#understand-the-css-box-model

What does * { box-sizing: border-box; } do? What are its advantages?

- By default, elements have box-sizing: content-box applied, and only the content size is being accounted for.
- box-sizing: border-box changes how the width and height of elements are being calculated, border and padding are also being included in the calculation.
- The height of an element is now calculated by the content's height + vertical padding + vertical border width.
- The width of an element is now calculated by the content's width + horizontal padding + horizontal border width.
- Taking into account paddings and borders as part of our box model resonates better with how designers actually imagine content in grids.

References

- https://www.paulirish.com/2012/box-sizing-border-box-ftw/

What is the CSS display property and can you give a few examples of its use?

- none - Displays an element as an inline element (like <span>). Any height and width properties will have no effect
- block - Displays an element as a block element (like <p>). It starts on a new line, and takes up the whole width
- contents - Makes the container disappear, making the child elements children of the element the next level up in the DOM
- flex - Displays an element as a block-level flex container
- inline
- inline-block - Displays an element as an inline-level block container. The element itself is formatted as an inline element, but you can apply height and width values
- initial - Sets this property to its default value
- inherit - Inherits this property from its parent element
- inline-flex - Displays an element as an inline-level flex container
- table - Let the element behave like a <table> element
- table-row - Let the element behave like a <tr> element none The element is completely removed
- table-cell - Let the element behave like a <td> element

What's the difference between inline and inline-block?

- inline-block - it brought a new way to create side by side boxes that collapse and wrap properly depending on the available space in the containing element. It makes layouts that were previously accomplished

105

with floats easier to create. No need to clear floats anymore.

- inline - the major difference is that inline-block allows to set a width and height on the element. Also, with display: inline, top and bottom margins & paddings are not respected, while with display: inline-block they are.

What's the difference between a relative, fixed, absolute and statically positioned element?

A positioned element is an element whose computed position property is either relative, absolute, fixed or sticky.

- static - The default position; the element will flow into the page as it normally would. The top, right, bottom, left and z-index properties do not apply.
- relative - The element's position is adjusted relative to itself, without changing layout (and thus leaving a gap for the element where it would have been had it not been positioned).
- absolute - The element is removed from the flow of the page and positioned at a specified position relative to its closest positioned ancestor if any, or otherwise relative to the initial containing block. Absolutely positioned boxes can have margins, and they do not collapse with any other margins. These elements do not affect the position of other elements.
- fixed - The element is removed from the flow of the page and positioned at a specified position relative to the viewport and doesn't move when scrolled.
- sticky - Sticky positioning is a hybrid of relative and fixed positioning. The element is treated as relative positioned until it crosses a specified threshold, at which point it is treated as fixed positioned.

References

106

- https://developer.mozilla.org/en/docs/Web/CSS/position

What existing CSS frameworks have you used locally, or in production? How would you change/improve them?

- **Bootstrap** - Slow release cycle. Bootstrap 4 has been in alpha for almost 2 years, it is very widely used.
- **Semantic UI** - Source code structure makes theme customization extremely hard to understand. Its unconventional theming system is a pain to customize. Hardcoded config path within the vendor library. Not well-designed for overriding variables unlike in Bootstrap.
- **Bulma** - A lot of non-semantic and superfluous classes and markup required. Not backward compatible. Upgrading versions breaks the app in subtle manners.
- **Basscss** - Great minimalist css library, I would add further plugins/component for elements like sticky navbar etc.

Have you played around with the new CSS Flexbox or Grid specs?

Yes. Flexbox is mainly meant for 1-dimensional layouts while Grid is meant for 2-dimensional layouts.

Flexbox solves many common problems in CSS, such as vertical centering of elements within a container, sticky footer, etc. Bootstrap and Bulma are based on Flexbox, and it is probably the recommended way to create layouts these days. Have tried Flexbox before but ran into some browser incompatibility issues (Safari) in using flex-grow, and I had to rewrite my code using inline-blocks and math to calculate the widths in percentages, it wasn't a nice experience.

Grid is by far the most intuitive approach for creating grid-based layouts (it better be!) but browser support is not wide at the moment.

References

- https://philipwalton.github.io/solved-by-flexbox/

Can you explain the difference between coding a website to be responsive versus using a mobile-first strategy?

Note that these two 2 approaches are not exclusive.

Making a website responsive means the some elements will respond by adapting its size or other functionality according to the device's screen size, typically the viewport width, through CSS media queries, for example, making the font size smaller on smaller devices.

```
@media (min-width: 601px) {
  .my-class {
    font-size: 24px;
  }
}


@media (max-width: 600px) {
  .my-class {
    font-size: 12px;
  }
}
```

A mobile-first strategy is also responsive, however it agrees we should default and define all the styles for mobile devices, and only add specific responsive rules to other devices later. Following the previous example:

```
.my-class {
  font-size: 12px;
}


@media (min-width: 600px) {
  .my-class {
    font-size: 24px;
  }
}
```

A mobile-first strategy has 2 main advantages:

- Better performance on mobile devices, since all the rules applied for them don't have to be validated against any media queries.
- Forces to write cleaner code in respect to responsive CSS rules.

Tailwindcss is a CSS framework that feels very mobile first.

How is responsive design different from adaptive design?

Both responsive and adaptive design attempt to optimize the user experience across different devices, adjusting for different viewport sizes, resolutions, usage contexts, control mechanisms, and so on.

Responsive design works on the principle of flexibility - a single fluid website that can look good on any device.

109

Responsive websites use media queries, flexible grids, and responsive images to create a user experience that flexes and changes based on a multitude of factors. Like a single ball growing or shrinking to fit through several different hoops.

Adaptive design is more like the modern definition of progressive enhancement. Instead of one flexible design, adaptive design detects the device and other features and then provides the appropriate feature and layout based on a predefined set of viewport sizes and other characteristics. The site detects the type of device used and delivers the pre-set layout for that device. Instead of a single ball going through several different-sized hoops, you'd have several different balls to use depending on the hoop size.

References

- https://developer.mozilla.org/en-US/docs/Archive/Apps/Design/UI_layout_basics/Responsive_design_versus_adaptive_design
- http://mediumwell.com/responsive-adaptive-mobile/
- https://css-tricks.com/the-difference-between-responsive-and-adaptive-design/

Have you ever worked with retina graphics? If so, when and what techniques did you use?

Retina is just a marketing term to refer to high resolution screens with a pixel ratio bigger than 1. The key thing to know is that using a pixel ratio means these displays are emulating a lower resolution screen in order to show elements with the same size. Nowadays we consider all mobile devices *retina* defacto displays.

Browsers by default render DOM elements according to the device resolution, except for images.

In order to have crisp, good-looking graphics that make the best of retina displays we need to use high resolution images whenever possible. However using always the highest resolution images will have an impact on performance as more bytes will need to be sent over the wire.

To overcome this problem, we can use responsive images, as specified in HTML5. It requires making available different resolution files of the same image to the browser and let it decide which image is best, using the html attribute srcset and optionally sizes, for instance:

```
<div responsive-background-image>
  <img
    src="/images/test-1600.jpg"
    sizes="
      (min-width: 768px) 50vw,
      (min-width: 1024px) 66vw,
      100vw"
    srcset="
      /images/test-400.jpg 400w,
      /images/test-800.jpg 800w,
      /images/test-1200.jpg 1200w
    "
  />
</div>
```

It is important to note that browsers which don't support HTML5's srcset (i.e. IE11) will ignore it and use src instead. If we really need to support IE11 and we want to provide this feature for performance reasons, we can use a JavaScript polyfill, e.g. Picturefill (link in the references).

For icons, I would also opt to use SVGs and icon fonts where possible, as they render very crisply regardless of resolution.

References

- https://css-tricks.com/responsive-images-youre-just-changing-resolutions-use-srcset
- http://scottjehl.github.io/picturefill/
- https://aclaes.com/responsive-background-images-with-srcset-and-sizes/

Is there any reason you'd want to use translate() instead of absolute positioning, or vice-versa? And why?

translate() is a value of CSS transform. Changing transform or opacity does not trigger browser reflow or repaint but does trigger compositions; whereas changing the absolute positioning triggers reflow. transform causes the browser to create a GPU layer for the element but changing absolute positioning properties uses the CPU. Hence translate() is more efficient and will result in shorter paint times for smoother animations.

When using translate(), the element still occupies its original space (sort of like position: relative), unlike in changing the absolute positioning.

References

- https://www.paulirish.com/2012/why-moving-elements-with-translate-is-better-than-posabs-topleft/

Bootstrap

Bootstrap is one of the most prominent front end framework used in the industry. A job position for a front end developer is very likely to require some basic understanding of it. Frequently asked Bootstrap questions:

What is Bootstrap? What is it used for?

Bootstrap is one of the most widely used front-end frameworks based on HTML, CSS, JavaScript. It was created by Twitter.

Bootstrap is used to build Responsive websites. Responsive Web Design enables the same page to fit well on different sized devices like mobile, tablet, desktop etc.

What is bootstrap grid system?

Bootstrap grid system is a structure to create layout of webpages. It provides a total of 12 columns which can be used as per the layout requirement.

Grid classes are the classes that are used to give the proper layout to the pages. Different classes are used as per the type of device.

In bootstrap there are four grid classes:

- **xs** - This is used for extra small display devices with the width of less than 768px.

- **sm** - This is used for small display devices with the width equal to or greater than 768px.
- **md** - This is used for medium display devices with the width equal to or greater than 992px.
- **lg** - This is used for large display devices with the width equal to or greater than 1200px.

What is the use of offset in bootstrap?

Offset is used to add margin, equivalent to the number of columns mentioned with offset. Margin is added on both the sides i.e. left and right. Like in the example below col-sm-offset-3 is used so it will create the margin i.e. equivalent to 3 columns.

```
<div class="col-sm-6 col-sm-offset-3">
</div>
```

What does img-responsive class do?

img-responsive is a bootstrap class which is used to create responsive images. It adjusts the image as per the size of the display. It applies three properties.

- display: block;
- max-width: 100%;
- height: auto;

How would you divide the page on a mobile device into two equal parts using grid classes?

Bootstrap class xs can be used to divide the display on small devices like mobile, as below:

```
<div class="col-xs-6">
   Left Half
```

```
</div>
<div class="col-xs-6">
  Right Half
</div>
```

What is the difference between .container and .container-fluid?

These are two bootstrap classes out of which .container has a specific margin and padding set on the left and right side while .container-fluid the latter has the full width.

What is affix?

Affix is a plugin which is used to fix or lock any element in a page as per the scroll position. Also it can be used to switch between fixed and movable state.

Chapter 7 - JavaScript

JavaScript is the the most popular programming language for web development. As per recent reports, JavaScript is currently being used by more than 94 percent of all the websites, and is becoming extremely popular on the server side too.

If you are new to JavaScript, learning the basics of JavaScript is a must. I recommend, like for the HTML & CSS topic, to sign up for freecodecamp and follow the JavaScript module.

It is important to have some basic understanding of both JavaScript on the front end and on the back end, even if you are applying for a jobs that don't put the emphasis on web development.

This chapter covers the most commonly used interview questions.

General

Explain event delegation

Event delegation is a technique involving adding event listeners to a parent element instead of adding them to the descendant elements. The listener will fire whenever the event is triggered on the descendant elements due to event bubbling up the DOM. The benefits of this technique are:

- Memory footprint goes down because only one single handler is needed on the parent element, rather than having to attach event handlers on each descendant.

- There is no need to unbind the handler from elements that are removed and to bind the event for new elements.

References

- https://davidwalsh.name/event-delegate
- https://stackoverflow.com/questions/1687296/what-is-dom-event-delegation

Explain how this works in JavaScript

There's no simple explanation for this; it is one of the most confusing concepts in JavaScript. A hand-wavey explanation is that the value of this depends on how the function is called. I have read many explanations on this online, and I found Arnav Aggrawal's explanation to be the clearest. The following rules are applied:

1. If the new keyword is used when calling the function, this inside the function is a brand new object.
2. If apply, call, or bind are used to call/create a function, this inside the function is the object that is passed in as the argument.
3. If a function is called as a method, such as obj.method()—this is the object that the function is a property of.
4. If a function is invoked as a free function invocation, meaning it was invoked without any of the conditions present above, this is the global object. In a browser, it is the window object. If in strict mode ('use strict'), this will be undefined instead of the global object.
5. If multiple of the above rules apply, the rule that is higher wins and will set the this value.
6. If the function is an ES2015 arrow function, it ignores all the rules above and receives the this value of its surrounding scope at the time it is created.

117

References

- https://codeburst.io/the-simple-rules-to-this-in-javascript-35d97f31bde3
- https://stackoverflow.com/a/3127440/1751946

Explain how prototypal inheritance works

This is an extremely common JavaScript interview question. All JavaScript objects have a prototype property, that is a reference to another object. When a property is accessed on an object and if the property is not found on that object, the JavaScript engine looks at the object's prototype, and the prototype's prototype and so on, until it finds the property defined on one of the prototypes or until it reaches the end of the prototype chain. This behavior simulates classical inheritance, but it is really more of delegation than inheritance.

References

- https://www.quora.com/What-is-prototypal-inheritance/answer/Kyle-Simpson
- https://davidwalsh.name/javascript-objects

What do you think of AMD vs CommonJS?

Both are ways to implement a module system, which was not natively present in JavaScript until ES2015 came along. CommonJS is synchronous while AMD (Asynchronous Module Definition) is obviously asynchronous. CommonJS is designed with server-side development in mind while AMD, with its support for asynchronous loading of modules, is more intended for browsers.

I find AMD syntax to be quite verbose and CommonJS is closer to the style you would write import statements in other languages. Most of the time, I find AMD unnecessary, because if you served all your JavaScript into one concatenated bundle file, you wouldn't benefit from the async loading properties. Also, CommonJS syntax is closer to Node style of writing modules and there is less context-switching overhead when switching between client side and server side JavaScript development.

I'm glad that with ES2015 modules, that has support for both synchronous and asynchronous loading, we can finally just stick to one approach. Although it hasn't been fully rolled out in browsers and in Node, we can always use transpilers to convert our code.

References

- https://auth0.com/blog/javascript-module-systems-showdown/
- https://stackoverflow.com/questions/16521471/relation-between-commonjs-amd-and-requirejs

Explain why the following doesn't work as an IIFE: function foo(){ }();. What needs to be changed to properly make it an IIFE?

IIFE stands for Immediately Invoked Function Expressions. The JavaScript parser reads function foo(){ }(); as function foo(){ } and ();, where the former is a function declaration and the latter (a pair of brackets) is an attempt at calling a function but there is no name specified, hence it throws Uncaught SyntaxError: Unexpected token).

Here are two ways to fix it that involves adding more brackets: (function foo(){ })() and (function foo(){ }()). These functions are not exposed in the global scope and you can even omit its name if you do not need to reference itself within the body.

You might also use void operator: void function foo(){ }();. Unfortunately, there is one issue with such approach. The evaluation of given expression is always undefined, so if your IIFE function returns anything, you can't use it. An example:

```
const foo = void (function bar() {
  return 'foo'
})();

console.log(foo); // undefined
```

References

- http://lucybain.com/blog/2014/immediately-invoked-function-expression/
- https://developer.mozilla.org/en-US/docs/Web/JavaScript/Reference/Operators/void

What's the difference between a variable that is: null, undefined or undeclared? How would you go about checking for any of these states?

Undeclared variables are created when you assign a value to an identifier that is not previously created using var, let or const. Undeclared variables will be defined globally, outside of the current scope. In strict mode, a ReferenceError will be thrown when you try to assign to an undeclared

120

variable. Undeclared variables are bad just like how global variables are bad. Avoid them at all cost! To check for them, wrap its usage in a try/catch block.

```javascript
function foo() {
  x = 1;
  // Throws a ReferenceError
  // in strict mode
}

foo();
console.log(x); // 1
```

A variable that is undefined is a variable that has been declared, but not assigned a value. It is of type undefined. If a function does not return any value as the result of executing it is assigned to a variable, the variable also has the value of undefined.

To check for it, compare using the strict equality (===) operator or typeof which will give the 'undefined' string. Note that you should not be using the abstract equality operator to check, as it will also return true if the value is null.

```javascript
var foo;
console.log(foo);
// undefined
console.log(foo === undefined);
// true
console.log(typeof foo === 'undefined');
// true

console.log(foo == null);
// true.
// Wrong, don't use this to check!
```

```
function bar() {}
var baz = bar();
console.log(baz);
// undefined
```

A variable that is null will have been explicitly assigned to the null value. It represents no value and is different from undefined in the sense that it has been explicitly assigned.

To check for null, simply compare using the strict equality operator. Note that like the above, you should not be using the abstract equality operator (==) to check, as it will also return true if the value is undefined.

```
var foo = null;
console.log(foo === null);
// true
console.log(typeof foo === 'object');
// true

console.log(foo == undefined);
// true. Wrong,
// don't use this to check!
```

As a personal habit, I never leave my variables undeclared or unassigned. I will explicitly assign null to them after declaring if I don't intend to use it yet. If you use a linter in your workflow, it will usually also be able to check that you are not referencing undeclared variables.

References

- https://stackoverflow.com/questions/15985875/effect-of-declared-and-undeclared-variables

- https://developer.mozilla.org/en/docs/Web/JavaScript/Reference/Global_Objects/undefined

What is a closure, and how/why would you use it?

A closure is the combination of a function and the lexical environment within which that function was declared. The word "lexical" refers to the fact that lexical scoping uses the location where a variable is declared within the source code to determine where that variable is available. Closures are functions that have access to the outer (enclosing) function's variables—scope chain even after the outer function has returned.

Why would you use one?

- Data privacy / emulating private methods with closures. Commonly used in the module pattern.
- Partial applications or currying.

References

- https://developer.mozilla.org/en-US/docs/Web/JavaScript/Closures
- https://medium.com/javascript-scene/master-the-javascript-interview-what-is-a-closure-b2f0d2152b36

Can you describe the main difference between a .forEach loop and a .map() loop and why you would pick one rather than the other?

To understand the differences between the two, let's look at what each function does.

forEach

- Iterates through the elements in an array.
- Executes a callback for each element.
- Does not return a value.

```
const a = [1, 2, 3];
const doubled = a.forEach(
  (num, index) => {
  // Do something with num and/or index.
  }
);

// doubled = undefined
```

map

- Iterates through the elements in an array.
- "Maps" each element to a new element by calling the function on each element, creating a new array as a result.

```
const a = [1, 2, 3];
const doubled = a.map(num => {
  return num * 2;
});

// doubled = [2, 4, 6]
```

The main difference between .forEach and .map() is that .map() returns a new array. If you need the result, but do not wish to mutate the original array, .map() is the clear choice. If you simply need to iterate over an array, forEach is a fine choice.

References

- https://codeburst.io/javascript-map-vs-foreach-f38111822c0f

What's a typical use case for anonymous functions?

They can be used in IIFEs to encapsulate some code within a local scope so that variables declared in it do not leak to the global scope.

```
(function() {
  // Some code here.
})();
```

As a callback that is used once and does not need to be used anywhere else. The code will seem more self-contained and readable when handlers are defined right inside the code calling them, rather than having to search elsewhere to find the function body.

```
setTimeout(function() {
  console.log('Hello world!');
}, 1000);
```

Arguments to functional programming constructs or Lodash (similar to callbacks).

```
const arr = [1, 2, 3];
const double = arr.map(function(el) {
  return el * 2;
});
console.log(double);
// [2, 4, 6]
```

References

- https://www.quora.com/What-is-a-typical-usecase-for-anonymous-functions
- https://stackoverflow.com/questions/10273185/what-are-the-benefits-to-using-anonymous-functions-instead-of-named-functions-fo

How do you organize your code? (module pattern, classical inheritance?)

In the past, I used Backbone for my models which encourages a more OOP approach, creating Backbone models and attaching methods to them.

The module pattern is still great, but these days, I use React/Redux which utilize a single-directional data flow based on Flux architecture. I would represent my app's models using plain objects and write utility pure functions to manipulate these objects. State is manipulated using actions and reducers like in any other Redux application.

I avoid using classical inheritance where possible.

What's the difference between host objects and native objects?

Native objects are objects that are part of the JavaScript language defined by the ECMAScript specification, such as String, Math, RegExp, Object, Function, etc.

Host objects are provided by the runtime environment (browser or Node), such as window, XMLHTTPRequest, etc.

References

126

- https://stackoverflow.com/questions/7614317/what-is-the-difference-between-native-objects-and-host-objects

Difference between: function Person(){}, var person = Person(), and var person = new Person()?

This question is pretty vague. My best guess at its intention is that it is asking about constructors in JavaScript. Technically speaking, function Person(){} is just a normal function declaration. The convention is to use PascalCase for functions that are intended to be used as constructors.

var person = Person() invokes the Person as a function, and not as a constructor. Invoking as such is a common mistake if it the function is intended to be used as a constructor. Typically, the constructor does not return anything, hence invoking the constructor like a normal function will return undefined and that gets assigned to the variable intended as the instance.

var person = new Person() creates an instance of the Person object using the new operator, which inherits from Person.prototype. An alternative would be to use Object.create, such as: Object.create(Person.prototype).

```
function Person(name) {
  this.name = name;
}

var person = Person('John');
console.log(person);
// undefined
console.log(person.name);
```

```
// Uncaught TypeError
// Cannot read property 'name'
// of undefined
```

```
var person = new Person('John');
console.log(person);
// Person { name: "John" }
console.log(person.name);
// "john"
```

References

- https://developer.mozilla.org/en-US/docs/Web/JavaScript/Reference/Operators/new

What's the difference between .call and .apply?

Both .call and .apply are used to invoke functions and the first parameter will be used as the value of this within the function. However, .call takes in comma-separated arguments as the next arguments while .apply takes in an array of arguments as the next argument. An easy way to remember this is C for call and comma-separated and A for apply and an array of arguments.

```
function add(a, b) {
  return a + b;
}
```

```
console.log(add.call(null, 1, 2));
// 3
console.log(add.apply(null, [1, 2]));
// 3
```

Explain Function.prototype.bind

Taken word-for-word from MDN:

> The bind() method creates a new function that, when called, has its this keyword set to the provided value, with a given sequence of arguments preceding any provided when the new function is called.

In my experience, it is most useful for binding the value of this in methods of classes that you want to pass into other functions. This is frequently done in React components.

References

- https://developer.mozilla.org/en/docs/Web/JavaScript/Reference/Global_objects/Function/bind

When would you use document.write()?

document.write() writes a string of text to a document stream opened by document.open(). When document.write() is executed after the page has loaded, it will call document.open which clears the whole document (<head> and <body> removed!) and replaces the contents with the given parameter value. Hence it is usually considered dangerous and prone to misuse.

References

- https://www.quirksmode.org/blog/archives/2005/06/three_javascrip_1.html
- https://github.com/h5bp/html5-boilerplate/wiki/Script-Loading-Techniques#documentwrite-script-tag

What's the difference between feature detection, feature inference, and using the UA string?

Feature Detection

Feature detection involves working out whether a browser supports a certain block of code, and running different code depending on whether it does (or doesn't), so that the browser can always provide a working experience rather crashing/erroring in some browsers. For example:

```
if ('geolocation' in navigator) {
  // Can use navigator.geolocation
} else {
  // Handle lack of feature
}
```

Modernizr is a great library to handle feature detection.

Feature Inference

Feature inference checks for a feature just like feature detection, but uses another function because it assumes it will also exist, e.g.:

```
if (document.getElementsByTagName) {
  element = document.getElementById(id);
}
```

This is not really recommended. Feature detection is more foolproof.

UA String

This is a browser-reported string that allows the network protocol peers to identify the application type, operating system, software vendor or software version of the requesting software user agent. It can be accessed via navigator.userAgent. However, the string is tricky to parse and can be spoofed. For example, Chrome reports both as Chrome and Safari. So to detect Safari you have to check for the Safari string and the absence of the Chrome string. Avoid this method.

References

- https://developer.mozilla.org/en-US/docs/Learn/Tools_and_testing/Cross_browser_testing/Feature_detection
- https://stackoverflow.com/questions/20104930/whats-the-difference-between-feature-detection-feature-inference-and-using-th
- https://developer.mozilla.org/en-US/docs/Web/HTTP/Browser_detection_using_the_user_agent

Explain Ajax in as much detail as possible

Ajax (asynchronous JavaScript and XML) is a set of web development techniques using many web technologies on the client side to create asynchronous web applications. With Ajax, web applications can send data to and retrieve from a server asynchronously (in the background) without interfering with the display and behavior of the existing page.

By decoupling the data interchange layer from the presentation layer, Ajax allows for web pages, and by extension web applications, to change content dynamically without the need to reload the entire page. In practice, modern implementations commonly substitute use JSON instead of XML, due to the advantages of JSON being native to JavaScript.

The XMLHttpRequest API is frequently used for the asynchronous communication or these days, the fetch API.

References

- https://en.wikipedia.org/wiki/Ajax_(programming)
- https://developer.mozilla.org/en-US/docs/AJAX

What are the advantages and disadvantages of using Ajax?

Advantages

- Better interactivity. New content from the server can be changed dynamically without the need to reload the entire page.
- Reduce connections to the server since scripts and stylesheets only have to be requested once.
- State can be maintained on a page. JavaScript variables and DOM state will persist because the main container page was not reloaded.

Disadvantages

- Dynamic webpages are harder to bookmark.
- Does not work if JavaScript has been disabled in the browser.
- Some webcrawlers do not execute JavaScript and would not see content that has been loaded by JavaScript.

Explain how JSONP works (and how it's not really Ajax)

JSONP (JSON with Padding) is a method commonly used to bypass the cross-domain policies in web browsers because Ajax requests from the current page to a cross-origin domain is not allowed.

JSONP works by making a request to a cross-origin domain via a <script> tag and usually with a callback query parameter, for example: https://ext.com?callback=printData. The server will then wrap the data within a function called print and return it to the client.

```
<!-- https://mydomain.com -->
<script>
  function printData(data) {
    console.log(
      `My name is ${data.name}!`
    );
  }
</script>

<script
  src="http://ext.com?callback=print">
</script>


// File loaded from
// https://ext.com?callback=print
print({ name: 'Yang Shun' });
```

The client has to have the printData function in its global scope and the function will be executed by the client when the response from the cross-origin domain is received.

JSONP can be unsafe and has some security implications. As JSONP is really JavaScript, it can do everything else JavaScript can do, so you need to trust the provider of the JSONP data.

These days, CORS is the recommended approach and JSONP is seen as a hack.

References

- https://stackoverflow.com/a/2067584/1751946

Have you ever used JavaScript templating? If so, what libraries have you used?

Yes. Handlebars, Underscore, Lodash, AngularJS, and JSX. Templating in AngularJS makes heavy use of strings in the directives and typos would go uncaught. JSX uses a different approach moving the template closer to JavaScript and there is barely any syntax to learn. Nowadays, one can even use ES2015 template string literals as a quick way for creating templates without relying on third-party code.

```
const template = `
  <div>My name is: ${name}</div>
`;
```

However, do be aware of a potential XSS in the above approach as the contents are not escaped for you, unlike in templating libraries.

Explain "hoisting"

Hoisting is a term used to explain the behavior of variable declarations in your code. Variables declared or initialized with the var keyword will have their declaration "moved" up to the top of the current scope, which we refer to as hoisting. However, only the declaration is hoisted, the assignment (if there is one), will stay where it is.

Note that the declaration is not actually moved - the JavaScript engine parses the declarations during compilation and becomes aware of declarations and their scopes. It is just easier to understand this behavior by visualizing the declarations as being hoisted to the top of their scope. Let's explain with a few examples.

```javascript
// var declarations
// are hoisted.
console.log(foo);
// undefined
var foo = 1;
console.log(foo);
// 1


// let/const declarations
// are NOT hoisted.
console.log(bar);
// ReferenceError:
// bar is not defined
let bar = 2;
console.log(bar);
// 2
```

Function declarations have the body hoisted while the function expressions (written in the form of variable declarations) only has the variable declaration hoisted.

```javascript
// Function Declaration
console.log(foo);
// [Function: foo]
foo();
// 'FOOOOO'
function foo() {
  console.log('FOOOOO');
}
console.log(foo);
// [Function: foo]


// Function Expression
console.log(bar);
// undefined
bar();
// Uncaught TypeError:
// bar is not a function
var bar = function() {
  console.log('BARRRR');
};
console.log(bar);
// [Function: bar]
```

Describe event bubbling

When an event triggers on a DOM element, it will attempt to handle the event if there is a listener attached, then the event is bubbled up to its parent and the same thing happens. This bubbling occurs up the element's ancestors all the way to the document. Event bubbling is the mechanism behind event delegation.

What's the difference between an "attribute" and a "property"?

Attributes are defined on the HTML markup but properties are defined on the DOM. To illustrate the difference, imagine we have this text field in our HTML: <input type="text" value="Hello">.

```
const input = document.querySelector(
  'input'
);
console.log(input.getAttribute(
  'value'
));
// Hello
console.log(input.value);
// Hello
```

But after you change the value of the text field by adding "World!" to it, this becomes:

```
console.log(input.getAttribute(
  'value'
));
// Hello
console.log(input.value);
// Hello World!
```

References

- https://stackoverflow.com/questions/6003819/properties-and-attributes-in-html

Why is extending built-in JavaScript objects not a good idea?

Extending a built-in/native JavaScript object means adding properties/functions to its prototype. While this may seem like a good idea at first, it is dangerous in practice. Imagine your code uses a few libraries that both extend the Array.prototype by adding the same contains method, the implementations will overwrite each other and your code will break if the behavior of these two methods is not the same.

The only time you may want to extend a native object is when you want to create a polyfill, essentially providing your own implementation for a method that is part of the JavaScript specification but might not exist in the user's browser due to it being an older browser.

References

- http://lucybain.com/blog/2014/js-extending-built-in-objects/

Difference between document load event and document DOMContentLoaded event?

The DOMContentLoaded event is fired when the initial HTML document has been completely loaded and parsed, without waiting for stylesheets, images, and subframes to finish loading.

window's load event is only fired after the DOM and all dependent resources and assets have loaded.

References

- https://developer.mozilla.org/en-US/docs/Web/Events/DOMContentLoaded
- https://developer.mozilla.org/en-US/docs/Web/Events/load

What is the difference between == and ===?

== is the abstract equality operator while === is the strict equality operator. The == operator will compare for equality after doing any necessary type conversions. The === operator will not do type conversion, so if two values are not the same type === will simply return false. When using ==, funky things can happen, such as:

```
1 == '1'; // true
1 == [1]; // true
1 == true; // true
0 == ''; // true
0 == '0'; // true
0 == false; // true
```

It's best to never use the == operator, except for convenience when comparing against null or undefined, where a == null will return true if a is null or undefined.

```
var a = null;
console.log(a == null);
// true
console.log(a == undefined);
// true
```

References

- https://stackoverflow.com/questions/359494/which-equals-operator-vs-should-be-used-in-javascript-comparisons

Explain the same-origin policy with regards to JavaScript

The same-origin policy prevents JavaScript from making requests across domain boundaries. An origin is defined as a combination of URI scheme, hostname, and port number. This policy prevents a malicious script on one page from obtaining access to sensitive data on another web page through that page's Document Object Model.

References

- https://en.wikipedia.org/wiki/Same-origin_policy

What is "use strict";? What are the advantages and disadvantages to using it?

'use strict' is a statement used to enable strict mode to entire scripts or individual functions. Strict mode is a way to opt into a restricted variant of JavaScript.

Advantages

- Makes it impossible to accidentally create global variables.
- Makes assignments which would otherwise silently fail to throw an exception.
- Makes attempts to delete undeletable properties throw (where before the attempt would simply have no effect).
- Requires that function parameter names be unique.
- this is undefined in the global context.
- It catches some common coding bloopers, throwing exceptions.
- It disables features that are confusing or poorly thought out.

Disadvantages

- Many missing features that some developers might be used to.
- No more access to function.caller and function.arguments.
- Concatenation of scripts written in different strict modes might cause issues.

Overall, I think the benefits outweigh the disadvantages, and I never had to rely on the features that strict mode blocks. I would recommend using strict mode.

References

- http://2ality.com/2011/10/strict-mode-hatred.html
- http://lucybain.com/blog/2014/js-use-strict/

Create a for loop that iterates up to 100 while outputting "fizz" at multiples of 3, "buzz" at multiples of 5 and "fizzbuzz" at multiples of 3 and 5.

Check out this version of FizzBuzz by Paul Irish.

```
for (let i = 1; i <= 100; i++) {
  let f = i % 3 == 0,
    b = i % 5 == 0;
  console.log(f ?
          (b ? 'FizzBuzz'
             : 'Fizz')
        : b ? 'Buzz'
          : i);
}
```

I would not advise you to write the above during interviews though. Just stick with the long but clear approach. For more wacky versions of FizzBuzz, check out the reference link below.

References

- https://gist.github.com/jaysonrowe/1592432

Why is it, in general, a good idea to leave the global scope of a website as-is and never touch it?

Every script has access to the global scope, and if everyone uses the global namespace to define their variables, collisions will likely occur. Use the module pattern (IIFEs) to encapsulate your variables within a local namespace.

Why would you use something like the load event? Does this event have disadvantages? Do you know any alternatives, and why would you use those?

The load event fires at the end of the document loading process. At this point, all of the objects in the document are in the DOM, and all the images, scripts, links and sub-frames have finished loading.

The DOM event DOMContentLoaded will fire after the DOM for the page has been constructed, but do not wait for other resources to finish loading. This is preferred in certain cases when you do not need the full page to be loaded before initializing.

References

- https://developer.mozilla.org/en-US/docs/Web/API/GlobalEventHandlers/onload

Explain what a single page app is and how to make it SEO-friendly

Web developers these days refer to the products they build as web apps, rather than websites. While there is no strict difference between the two terms, web apps tend to be highly interactive and dynamic, allowing the user to perform actions and receive a response to their action. Traditionally, the browser receives HTML from the server and renders it. When the user navigates to another URL, a full-page refresh is required and the server sends fresh new HTML to the new page. This is called server-side rendering.

However, in modern SPAs, client-side rendering is used instead. The browser loads the initial page from the server, along with the scripts (frameworks, libraries, app code) and stylesheets required for the whole app. When the user navigates to other pages, a page refresh is not triggered. The URL of the page is updated via the HTML5 History API. New data required for the new page, usually in JSON format, is retrieved by the browser via AJAX requests to the server. The SPA then dynamically updates the page with the data via JavaScript, which it has already downloaded in the initial page load. This model is similar to how native mobile apps work.

The benefits

- The app feels more responsive and users do not see the flash between page navigations due to full-page refreshes.
- Fewer HTTP requests are made to the server, as the same assets do not have to be downloaded again for each page load.
- Clear separation of the concerns between the client and the server; you can easily build new clients for different platforms (e.g. mobile, chatbots, smart watches) without having to modify the server code.

You can also modify the technology stack on the client and server independently, as long as the API contract is not broken.

The downsides

- Heavier initial page load due to the loading of framework, app code, and assets required for multiple pages.
- There's an additional step to be done on your server which is to configure it to route all requests to a single entry point and allow client-side routing to take over from there.
- SPAs are reliant on JavaScript to render content, but not all search engines execute JavaScript during crawling, and they may see empty content on your page. This inadvertently hurts the Search Engine Optimization (SEO) of your app. However, most of the time, when you are building apps, SEO is not the most important factor, as not all the content needs to be indexable by search engines. To overcome this, you can either server-side render your app or use services such as Prerender to "render your javascript in a browser, save the static HTML, and return that to the crawlers".

References

- https://github.com/grab/front-end-guide
- http://stackoverflow.com/questions/21862054/single-page-app-advantages-and-disadvantages
- http://blog.isquaredsoftware.com/presentations/2016-10-revolution-of-web-dev/
- https://medium.freecodecamp.com/heres-why-client-side-rendering-won-46a349fadb52

What is your experience with Promises and/or their polyfills?

A promise is an object that may produce a single value sometime in the future: either a resolved value or a reason that it's not resolved (e.g., a network error occurred). A promise may be in one of 3 possible states: fulfilled, rejected, or pending. Promise users can attach callbacks to handle the fulfilled value or the reason for rejection.

Some common polyfills are $.deferred, Q and Bluebird but not all of them comply with the specification. ES2015 supports Promises out of the box and polyfills are typically not needed these days.

References

- https://medium.com/javascript-scene/master-the-javascript-interview-what-is-a-promise-27fc71e77261

What are the pros and cons of using Promises instead of callbacks?

Pros

- Avoid callback hell which can be unreadable.
- Makes it easy to write sequential asynchronous code that is readable with .then().
- Makes it easy to write parallel asynchronous code with Promise.all().

Cons

- Slightly more complex code (debatable).
- In older browsers where ES2015 is not supported, you need to load a polyfill in order to use it.

What are some of the advantages/disadvantages of writing JavaScript code in a language that compiles/transpile to JavaScript?

Some examples of languages that compile/transpile to JavaScript include CoffeeScript, TypeScript, Elm, ClojureScript, and PureScript.

Advantages

- Fixes some of the longstanding problems in JavaScript and discourages JavaScript anti-patterns.
- Enables you to write shorter code, by providing some syntactic sugar on top of JavaScript, which I think ES5 lacks.
- Static types can help (in the case of TypeScript) for large projects that need to be maintained over time.

Disadvantages

- Require a build/compile process as browsers only run JavaScript and your code will need to be compiled into JavaScript before being served to browsers.
- Debugging can be a pain if your source maps do not map nicely to your pre-compiled source.
- Many developers are not familiar with these languages and will need to learn it. There's a ramp up cost involved.
- Smaller community (depends on the language), which means resources, tutorials, libraries, and tooling would be harder to find.
- IDE/editor support might be lacking.

Practically, ES2015 has vastly improved JavaScript and made it much nicer to write.

References

- https://softwareengineering.stackexchange.com/questions/72569/what-are-the-pros-and-cons-of-coffeescript

What tools and techniques do you use for debugging JavaScript code?

- JavaScript
  - Chrome Devtools
  - Debugger statements
  - Good old console.log
- React and Redux
  - React Devtools
  - Redux Devtools

References

- https://hackernoon.com/twelve-fancy-chrome-devtools-tips-dc1e39d10d9d
- https://raygun.com/blog/javascript-debugging/

What language constructions do you use for iterating over object properties and array items?

For objects

- **for loops** - However, this will also iterate through its inherited properties, and you will add an obj.hasOwnProperty(property) check before using it.
- **Object.keys()** - It is a static method that will lists all enumerable properties of the object.
- **Object.getOwnPropertyNames()** - It is also a static method, it will lists all enumerable and non-enumerable properties of the object that you pass it.

For arrays

- for loops - for (var i = 0; i < arr.length; i++). The common pitfall here is that var is in the function scope and not the block scope and most of the time you would want block scoped iterator variable. ES2015 introduces let which has block scope and it is recommended to use that instead. So this becomes: for (let i = 0; i < arr.length; i++).
- forEach - arr.forEach(function (el, index) { ... }). This construct can be more convenient at times because you do not have to use the index if all you need is the array elements. There are also the every and some methods which will allow you to terminate the iteration early.

Most of the time, I would prefer the .forEach method, but it really depends on what you are trying to do. for loops allow more flexibility, such as prematurely terminate the loop using break or incrementing the iterator more than once per loop.

Explain the difference between synchronous and asynchronous functions

Synchronous functions are blocking while asynchronous functions are not. In synchronous functions, statements complete before the next statement is run. In this case, the program is evaluated exactly in order of the statements and execution of the program is paused if one of the statements take a very long time.

Asynchronous functions usually accept a callback as a parameter and execution continue on the next line immediately after the asynchronous function is invoked. The callback is only invoked when the asynchronous operation is complete and the call stack is empty.

Heavy duty operations such as loading data from a web server or querying a database should be done asynchronously so that the main thread can continue executing other operations instead of blocking until that long operation to complete (in the case of browsers, the UI will freeze).

What is event loop? What is the difference between call stack and task queue?

The event loop is a single-threaded loop that monitors the call stack and checks if there is any work to be done in the task queue. If the call stack is empty and there are callback functions in the task queue, a function is dequeued and pushed onto the call stack to be executed.

If you haven't already checked out Philip Robert's talk on the Event Loop, you should. It is one of the most viewed videos on JavaScript.

References

- https://2014.jsconf.eu/speakers/philip-roberts-what-the-heck-is-the-event-loop-anyway.html
- http://theproactiveprogrammer.com/javascript/the-javascript-event-loop-a-stack-and-a-queue/

Explain the differences on the usage of foo between function foo() {} and var foo = function() {}

The former is a function declaration while the latter is a function expression. The key difference is that function declarations have its body hoisted but the bodies of function expressions are not (they have the same hoisting behavior as variables). For more explanation on hoisting, refer to the question above on hoisting.

If you try to invoke a function expression before it is defined, you will get an Uncaught TypeError: XXX is not a function error.

Function Declaration

```
foo(); // 'FOOOOO'
function foo() {
  console.log('FOOOOO');
}
```

Function Expression

```
foo();
// Uncaught TypeError:
// foo is not a function
var foo = function() {
  console.log('FOOOOO');
};
```

References

- https://developer.mozilla.org/en-US/docs/Web/JavaScript/Reference/Statements/function

What are the differences between variables created using let, var or const?

Variables declared using the var keyword are scoped to the function in which they are created, or if created outside of any function, to the global object. let and const are *block scoped*, meaning they are only accessible within the nearest set of curly braces (function, if-else block, or for-loop).

```javascript
function foo() {
  // All variables are
  // accessible within functions.
  var bar = 'bar';
  let baz = 'baz';
  const qux = 'qux';

  console.log(bar); // bar
  console.log(baz); // baz
  console.log(qux); // qux
}

console.log(bar);
// ReferenceError:
// bar is not defined
console.log(baz);
// ReferenceError:
// baz is not defined
console.log(qux);
// ReferenceError:
// qux is not defined

if (true) {
  var bar = 'bar';
  let baz = 'baz';
  const qux = 'qux';
}

// var declared variables
```

```javascript
// are accessible anywhere
// in the function scope.
console.log(bar); // bar
// let and const defined
// variables are not
// accessible outside
// of the block they
// were defined in.
console.log(baz);
// ReferenceError:
// baz is not defined
console.log(qux);
// ReferenceError:
// qux is not defined
```

var allows variables to be hoisted, meaning they can be referenced in code before they are declared. let and const will not allow this, instead throwing an error.

```javascript
console.log(foo);
// undefined

var foo = 'foo';


console.log(baz);
// ReferenceError:
// can't access lexical
// declaration 'baz'
// before initialization

let baz = 'baz';


console.log(bar);
// ReferenceError:
// can't access lexical
// declaration 'bar'
```

```
// before initialization

const bar = 'bar';
```

Redeclaring a variable with var will not throw an error, but 'let' and 'const' will.

```
var foo = 'foo';
var foo = 'bar';
console.log(foo);
// "bar"

let baz = 'baz';
let baz = 'qux';
// Uncaught SyntaxError:
// Identifier 'baz' has
// already been declared
```

let and const differ in that let allows reassigning the variable's value while const does not.

```
// This is fine.
let foo = 'foo';
foo = 'bar';

// This causes an exception.
const baz = 'baz';
baz = 'qux';
```

References

- https://developer.mozilla.org/en-US/docs/Web/JavaScript/Reference/Statements/let

- https://developer.mozilla.org/en-US/docs/Web/JavaScript/Reference/Statements/var
- https://developer.mozilla.org/en-US/docs/Web/JavaScript/Reference/Statements/const

What are the differences between ES6 class and ES5 function constructors?

Let's first look at some examples:

```js
// ES5 Function Constructor
function Person(name) {
  this.name = name;
}
```

```js
// ES6 Class
class Person {
  constructor(name) {
    this.name = name;
  }
}
```

For simple constructors, they look pretty similar.

The main difference in the constructor comes when using inheritance. If we want to create a Student class that subclasses Person and add a studentId field, this is what we have to do in addition to the above.

```js
// ES5 Function Constructor
function Student(name, studentId) {
  // Call constructor of superclass
  // to initialize superclass-derived
  // members.
```

```
  Person.call(this, name);

  // Initialize subclass's
  // own members.
  this.studentId = studentId;
}


Student.prototype = Object.create(
  Person.prototype
);
Student.prototype.constructor = Student;

// ES6 Class
class Student extends Person {
  constructor(name, studentId) {
    super(name);
    this.studentId = studentId;
  }
}
```

It's much more verbose to use inheritance in ES5 and the ES6 version is easier to understand and remember.

References

- https://developer.mozilla.org/en-US/docs/Learn/JavaScript/Objects/Inheritance
- https://eli.thegreenplace.net/2013/10/22/classical-inheritance-in-javascript-es5

What is the definition of a higher-order function?

A higher-order function is any function that takes one or more functions as arguments, which it uses to operate on some data, and/or returns a function as a result. Higher-order functions are meant to abstract some operation that is performed repeatedly.

The classic example of this is map, which takes an array and a function as arguments. map then uses this function to transform each item in the array, returning a new array with the transformed data. Other popular examples in JavaScript are forEach, filter, and reduce.

A higher-order function doesn't just need to be manipulating arrays as there are many use cases for returning a function from another function. Function.prototype.bind is one such example in JavaScript.

Map

Let say we have an array of names which we need to transform each string to uppercase.

```
const names = ['irish', 'daisy', 'anna'];
```

The imperative way will be as such:

```
const transformNamesToUppercase =
function(names) {
  const results = [];
  for (let i = 0; i < names.length; i++) {
    results.push(names[i].toUpperCase());
  }
  return results;
};
transformNamesToUppercase(names);
// ['IRISH', 'DAISY', 'ANNA']
```

Use .map(transformerFn) makes the code shorter and more declarative.

```
const transformNamesToUppercase =
function(names) {
  return names.map(
    name => name.toUpperCase()
  );
};
transformNamesToUppercase(names);
// ['IRISH', 'DAISY', 'ANNA']
```

References

- https://medium.com/javascript-scene/higher-order-functions-composing-software-5365cf2cbe99
- https://hackernoon.com/effective-functional-javascript-first-class-and-higher-order-functions-713fde8df50a
- https://eloquentjavascript.net/05_higher_order.html

Can you give an example for destructuring an object or an array?

Destructuring is an expression available in ES6 which enables a succinct and convenient way to extract values of Objects or Arrays and place them into distinct variables.

Array destructuring

```
// Variable assignment.
const foo = ['one', 'two', 'three'];

const [one, two, three] = foo;
```

```
console.log(one);
// "one"
console.log(two);
// "two"
console.log(three);
// "three"


// Swapping variables
let a = 1;
let b = 3;


[a, b] = [b, a];
console.log(a); // 3
console.log(b); // 1
```

Object destructuring

```
// Variable assignment.
const o = { p: 42, q: true };
const { p, q } = o;


console.log(p); // 42
console.log(q); // true
```

References

- https://developer.mozilla.org/en-US/docs/Web/JavaScript/Reference/Operators/Destructuring_assignment
- https://ponyfoo.com/articles/es6-destructuring-in-depth

Can you give an example of a curry function and why this syntax offers an advantage?

Currying is a pattern where a function with more than one parameter is broken into multiple functions that, when called in series, will accumulate all of the required parameters one at a time. This technique can be useful for making code written in a functional style easier to read and compose.

It's important to note that for a function to be curried, it needs to start out as one function, then broken out into a sequence of functions that each accepts one parameter.

```
function curry(fn) {
  if (fn.length === 0) {
    return fn;
  }

  function _curried(depth, args) {
    return function(newArgument) {
      if (depth - 1 === 0) {
        return fn(...args,
              newArgument);
      }
      return _curried(depth - 1,
            [...args, newArgument]);
    };
  }

  return _curried(fn.length, []);
}

function add(a, b) {
  return a + b;
}

var curriedAdd = curry(add);
```

```
var addFive = curriedAdd(5);

var result = [0, 1, 2, 3, 4, 5]
    .map(addFive);
    // [5, 6, 7, 8, 9, 10]
```

References

- https://hackernoon.com/currying-in-js-d9ddc64f162e

What are the benefits of using spread syntax and how is it different from rest syntax?

ES6's spread syntax is very useful when coding in a functional paradigm as we can easily create copies of arrays or objects without resorting to Object.create, slice, or a library function. This language feature is used often in Redux and rx.js projects.

```
function putDookieInAnyArray(arr) {
    return [...arr, 'dookie'];
}

const result = putDookieInAnyArray(
    ['I', 'really', "don't", 'like']
);
// ["I", "really", "don't",
//   "like", "dookie"]

const person = {
    name: 'Todd',
    age: 29
};
```

```
const copyOfTodd = { ...person };
```

ES6's rest syntax offers a shorthand for including an arbitrary number of arguments to be passed to a function. It is like an inverse of the spread syntax, taking data and stuffing it into an array rather than unpacking an array of data, and it works in function arguments, as well as in array and object destructuring assignments.

```
function addFiveToABunchOfNumbers(
  ...numbers
) {
  return numbers.map(x => x + 5);
}

const result = addFiveToABunchOfNumbers(
  4, 5, 6, 7, 8, 9, 10
); // [9, 10, 11, 12, 13, 14, 15]

const [a, b, ...rest] = [1, 2, 3, 4];
// a: 1, b: 2, rest: [3, 4]

const { e, f, ...others } = {
  e: 1,
  f: 2,
  g: 3,
  h: 4
};
// e: 1, f: 2, others: { g: 3, h: 4 }
```

References

- https://developer.mozilla.org/en-US/docs/Web/JavaScript/Reference/Operators/Spread_syntax
- https://developer.mozilla.org/en-US/docs/Web/JavaScript/Reference/Functions/rest_parameters
- https://developer.mozilla.org/en-US/docs/Web/JavaScript/Reference/Operators/Destructuring_assignment

How can you share code between files?

This depends on the JavaScript environment.

On the client (browser environment), as long as the variables/functions are declared in the global scope (window), all scripts can refer to them. Alternatively, adopt the Asynchronous Module Definition (AMD) via RequireJS for a more modular approach.

On the server (Node.js), the common way has been to use CommonJS. Each file is treated as a module and it can export variables and functions by attaching them to the module.exports object.

ES2015 defines a module syntax which aims to replace both AMD and CommonJS. This will eventually be supported in both browser and Node environments.

References

- http://requirejs.org/docs/whyamd.html
- https://nodejs.org/docs/latest/api/modules.html
- http://2ality.com/2014/09/es6-modules-final.html

Why would someone want to create static class members?

Static class members (properties/methods) are not tied to a specific instance of a class and have the same value regardless of which instance is referring to it. Static properties are typically configuration variables and static methods are usually pure utility functions which do not depend on the state of the instance.

References

- https://stackoverflow.com/questions/21155438/whe n-to-use-static-variables-methods-and-when-to-use-instance-variables-methods

Node.js

What is Node.js? What is it used for?

Node.js is a run-time JavaScript environment built on top of Chrome's V8 engine. It uses an event-driven, non-blocking I/O model. It is lightweight and efficient. Node.js has a package ecosystem called npm.

Node.js can be used to build different types of applications such as web application, real-time chat application, REST API server, etc. However, it is mainly used to build network programs like web servers, similar to PHP, Java, or ASP.NET. Node.js was developed by Ryan Dahl in 2009.

What is NPM?

NPM (Node package Manager) is a package, or dependency management tool that ships with node.js. It also referes to the online repository.

- Online repository for Node.js packages
- Command line utility for installing packages, version management and dependency management of Node.js packages.

What is package.json? What is it used for?

This file holds various metadata information about the Node.js project. It is used to give information to npm that allows it to identify the project as well as handle the project's dependencies.

Some of the fields are: name, name, description, author and dependencies.

When one installs the project through npm, all the dependencies listed will be installed locally, in the ./node_modules directory.

Does Node.js support multiple threads?

Node.js, in its essence, is a single thread process. It does not expose child threads and thread management methods to the developer. Technically, Node.js does spawn child threads for certain tasks such as asynchronous I/O, but these run behind the scenes and do not execute any application JavaScript code, nor block the main event loop.

If threading support is desired in a Node.js application, there are tools available to enable it, such as the ChildProcess module.

How does Node.js support multi-processor platforms, and does it fully utilize all processor resources?

Since Node.js is by default a single thread application, it will run on a single processor core and will not take full advantage of multiple core resources.

However, Node.js provides support for deployment on multiple-core systems, to take greater advantage of the hardware. The Cluster module is one of the core Node.js modules and it allows running multiple Node.js worker processes that will share the same port. External process managers are also available, such as PM2 or forever

How would you debug an application in Node.js?

Node.js includes a debugging utility called <u>debugger</u>. To enable it one can start Node.js with the debug argument followed by the path to the script to debug.

Inserting the statement debugger; into the source code of a script will enable a breakpoint at that position in the code, e.g:

```
setTimeout(() => {
  debugger;
  console.log('world');
}, 1000);
console.log('hello');
```

React.js

What is React?

Created by Facebook, React is a declarative, efficient, and flexible front end JavaScript framework for building user interfaces. It lets you compose complex UIs from small and isolated pieces of code called "components".

How does React work?

React creates a virtual DOM. When state changes in a component it firstly runs a "diffing" algorithm, which identifies what has changed in the virtual DOM. The second step is reconciliation, where it updates the DOM with the results of diff.

What are the advantages of using React?

- It is easy to know how a component is rendered, we just need to look at the render function.
- JSX makes it easy to read the code of our components. It is also really easy to see the layout, or how components are plugged/combined with each other.
- React can render on the server-side. This enables improves SEO and performance.
- Component based, makes the code easy to test.
- One can couple React with many other libraries, it is only a view layer.

What is the difference between a Presentational component and a Container component?

Presentational components are concerned with how things look. They generally receive data and callbacks exclusively via props. These components rarely have their own state, but when they do it generally concerns UI state, as opposed to data state.

Container components are more concerned with how things work. These components provide the data and behavior to presentational or other container components. They call Flux actions and provide these as callbacks to the presentational components. They are also often stateful as they serve as data sources.

What are the differences between a class component and functional component?

- Class components allows us to use additional features such as local state and lifecycle hooks. Also, to enable our component to have direct access to our store and thus holds state.
- When our component just receives props and renders them to the page, this is a 'stateless component', for which a pure function can be used. These are also called dumb components or presentational components.

What is the difference between state and props?

The state is a data structure that starts with a default value when a Component mounts. It may be mutated across time, mostly as a result of user events.

Props (short for properties) are a Component's configuration. They are received from above and immutable as far as the Component receiving them is concerned. A Component cannot change its props, but it is responsible for putting together the props of its child

Components. Props do not have to just be data - callback functions may be passed in as props.

Name the different lifecycle methods

- componentWillMount- this is most commonly used for App configuration in our root component.
- componentDidMount - here we want to do all the setup we couldn't do without a DOM, and start getting all the data we need. Also if we want to set up eventListeners etc. this lifecycle hook is a good place to do that.
- componentWillReceiveProps - this lifecyclye acts on particular prop changes to trigger state transitions.
- shouldComponentUpdate - if we're worried about wasted renders shouldComponentUpdate is a great place to improve performance as it allows us to prevent a rerender if component receives new prop. shouldComponentUpdate should always return a booleanand based on what this is will determine if the component is rerendered or not.
- componentWillUpdate - rarely used. It can be used instead of componentWillReceiveProps on a component that also has shouldComponentUpdate (but no access to previous props).
- componentDidUpdate - also commonly used to update the DOM in response to prop or state changes.
- componentWillUnmount - here we can cancel any outgoing network requests, or remove all event listeners associated with the component.

Where in a React component should you make an AJAX request?

componentDidMount is where an AJAX request should be made in a React component. This method will be executed when the component "mounts" (is added to the DOM) for the first time. This method is only executed once during the component's life.

Importantly, we can't guarantee the AJAX request will have resolved before the component mounts. If it doesn't, that would mean that we'd be trying to setState on an unmounted component, which would not work. Making our AJAX request in componentDidMount will guarantee that there's a component to update.

What are controlled components?

In HTML, form elements such as <input>, <textarea>, and <select> typically maintain their own state and update it based on user input. When a user submits a form the values from the aforementioned elements are sent with the form.

With React, it works differently. The component containing the form will keep track of the value of the input in it's state and will re-render the component each time the callback function e.g. onChange is fired as the state will be updated. An input form element whose value is controlled by React in this way is called a "controlled component".

What are refs used for in React?

Refs are used to get reference to a DOM node or an instance of a component in React. Good examples of when to use refs are for managing focus/text selection, triggering imperative animations, or integrating with third-party DOM libraries. We should avoid using string refs and inline ref callbacks. Callback refs are advised by React.

What is a higher order component?

A higher-order component is a function that takes a component and returns a new component. HOC's allow code reuse, logic and bootstrap abstraction. The most common is probably Redux's connect function. Beyond simply sharing utility libraries and simple composition, HOCs are the best way to share behavior between React Components. If we find ourself writing a lot of code in different places that does the same thing, we may be able to refactor that code into a reusable HOC.

What advantages are there in using arrow functions?

- Scope safety: Until arrow functions, every new function defined its own this value (a new object in the case of a constructor, undefined in strict mode function calls, the base object if the function is called as an "object method", etc.). An arrow function does not create its own this, the this value of the enclosing execution context is used.
- Compactness: Arrow functions are easier to read and write.
- Clarity: When almost everything is an arrow function, any regular function immediately sticks out for defining the scope. A developer can always look up the next-higher function statement to see what the thisObject is.

Why is it advised to pass a callback function to setState as opposed to an object?

Because this.props and this.state may be updated asynchronously, we should not rely on their values for calculating the next state.

What is the alternative of binding this in the constructor?

One can use property initializers to correctly bind callbacks. This is enabled by default in create react app. An arrow function could be used in the callback but the problem would be that a new callback gets created each time the component renders.

How would you prevent a component from rendering?

Returning null from a component's render method means nothing will be displayed, but it does not affect the firing of the component's lifecycle methods.

If the amount of times the component re-renders is an issue, there are two options available. Manually implementing a check in shouldComponentUpdate lifecycle method hook.

```
shouldComponentUpdate(nProps, nState){
  // Do some check here
  return resultOFCheckAsBoolean
}
```

Or using React.PureComponent instead of React.Component React.PureComponent implements shouldComponentUpdate() with a shallow prop and state comparison. This avoid re-rendering the component with the same props and state.

When rendering a list what is a key and what is it's purpose?

Keys help React identify which items have changed, are added, or are removed. Keys should be given to the elements inside the array to give the elements a stable identity. The best way to pick a key is to use a string that uniquely identifies a list item among its siblings.

Most often one would use IDs from the data as keys. When we don't have stable IDs for rendered items, we may use the item index as a key as a last resort. It is not recommend to use indexes for keys if the items can reorder.

What is the purpose of super(props)?

A child class constructor cannot make use of this until super() has been called. Also, ES2015 class constructors have to call super() if they are subclasses. The reason for passing props to super() is to enable access to this.props in the constructor.

What is JSX?

JSX is a syntax extension to JavaScript and comes with the full power of JavaScript. JSX produces React "elements". One can embed any JavaScript expression in JSX by wrapping it in curly braces. After compilation, JSX expressions become regular JavaScript objects. This means that we can use JSX inside if statements and for loops, assign it to variables, accept it as arguments, and return it from functions.

What is equivalent of the following using React.createElement?

```
const element =
    <h1 className="greeting">
      Hello, world!
    </h1>;
```

Answer

```
const element =
  React.createElement(
    'h1',
    { className: 'greeting' },
    'Hello, world!'
  );
```

What is Children?

In JSX expressions that contain both an opening tag and a closing tag, the content between those tags is passed to components automatically as a special prop: props.children.

There are a number of methods available in the React API to work with this prop. These include React.Children.map, React.Children.forEach, React.Children.count, React.Children.only, React.Children.toArray.

What is state in react?

State is similar to props, but it is private and fully controlled by the component. State is essentially an object that holds data and determines how the component renders and behaves.

What is redux?

The basic idea of redux is that the entire application state is kept in a single store. The store is simply a JavaScript object. The only way to change the state is by firing actions from your application and then writing reducers for these actions that modify the state. The entire state transition is kept inside reducers and should not have any side-effects.

What is a store in redux?

The store is a JavaScript object that holds the application state. Along with this it also has the following responsibilities:

- Allows access to state via getState();
- Allows state to be updated via dispatch(action);
- Registers listeners via subscribe(listener);
- Handles unregistering of listeners via the function returned by subscribe(listener).

What is an action?

Actions are plain JavaScript objects. They must have a type indicating the type of action being performed. In essence, actions are payloads of information that send data from your application to your store.

What is a reducer?

A reducer is simply a pure function that takes the previous state and an action, and returns the next state.

What is Redux Thunk used for?

Redux thunk is middleware that allows writing action creators that return a function instead of an action. The thunk can then be used to delay the dispatch of an action if a certain condition is met. This allows handling the asynchronous dispatching of actions.

What is a pure function?

A pure function is a function that doesn't depend on and doesn't modify the states of variables out of its scope. Essentially, this means that a pure function will always return the same result when given the same input parameters.

jQuery

What is jQuery?

jQuery is a cross-browser lightweight JavaScript library. It is designed to make navigation to any element easier and adding/invoking event handlers on the DOM. It assists handling client-side events, enable visual effects like animation, and make it easier to use Ajax in a web application.

What are the main features of jQuery

- Cross-browser support and detection.
- AJAX functions
- CSS functions
- DOM manipulation
- DOM transversal
- Attribute manipulation
- Event detection and handling.
- JavaScript animation
- Offers plugins for pre-built user interfaces, advanced animations, form validation, etc.
- Extensible plugin system.

What are selectors?

The basic operation in jQuery is selecting an element in the DOM. This is done with the help of the $() construct with a string parameter containing any CSS selector expression. $() will return zero or more DOM elements on which we can apply an effect or style.

Some selector types

- Element ID
- CSS Name

- Tag Name
- DOM hierarchy

How to use jQuery selectors?

A selector starts with $(). In the parentheses may be an element, a class or an ID.

Example

```
<div class=""leftBorder"">
  Bordered div on the Left
</div>
<div id=""leftPanel"">
  Panel div on the left
</div>
```

For the HTML above, jQuery syntax (for selectors) could be:

```
$("div")
  .action$(".leftBorder")
  .action
$("#leftPanel").action
```

This examples illustrates the following selector types: class selector and ID selector.

Which is the fastest selector in jQuery?

ID and Element selectors are the fastest in jQuery.

What is difference between prop and attr?

jQuery.attr() gets the value of an attribute for the first element in the set of matched elements.

Whereas jQuery.prop() gets the value of a property for the first element in the set of matched elements.

What is has() in JQuery?

has() is selection filter, it checks if a DOM element 'Has Something'. If we want to traverse the DOM and check if a div has the list tag (ol) then we can easily filter/check with the following code:

```
JQuery('div').has('ol');
```

The above code would select all elements having ol.

What is $(document).ready()?

$(document).ready() indicates that code in it needs to be executed once the DOM got loaded. It won't wait for the images to load for executing the jQuery script.

What is the difference between $(window).load and $(document).ready function in jQuery?

$(window).load is an event that fires when the DOM and all the content (everything) on the page is fully loaded.

What is the use of the each function in jQuery?

Each function is used to iterate each and every element of an object. It is used to loop DOM elements, arrays and the object properties.

What is jQuery.noConflict?

jQuery no-conflict is an option given by jQuery to overcome conflicts between different js frameworks or libraries. When one uses jQuery no-conflict mode, it replaces the $ to a new variable and assigns to jQuery some other JavaScript libraries.

Name a few common jQuery events?

- **click()** - Raises when an element is clicked
- **dblclick()** - Raises when any element is double-clicked
- **mouseenter()** - Raises when the mouse pointer enters in element
- **mouseleave()** - Raises when the mouse pointer leaves an element
- **mousedown()** - Raises when mouse pointer clicked down on element
- **mouseup()** - Raises when mouse pointer clicked and release on element
- **focus()** - Raises when element got focus

What is chaining in jQuery?

Chaining is a powerful feature of jQuery. Chaining means specifying multiple functions and/or selectors to an element.

Chaining reduces the code segment and keeps it clean and easy to understand. Generally, chaining uses the jQuery built in functions that makes compilation a bit faster.

The verbose code below:

```
$("#div1").text(div 1");
$("#div1").css("color", "red");
$("#div1").removeClass("cls");
```

With chaining, becomes:

```
$("#div1")
  .text(div 1")
  .css("color", "red")
  .removeClass("cls");
```

What is the use of jQuery.ajax method()?

The ajax() method is used to do an AJAX (asynchronous HTTP) request. It provides more control of the data sending and on response data. It allows the handling of errors that occur during a call and the data if the call to the ajax page is successful.

Some parameters of the ajax method:

- **type** - Specifies the type of request (GET or POST).
- **url** - Specifies the URL to send the request to. The default is the current page.
- **ontentType** - The content type used when sending data to the server. The default is application/x-www-form-urlencoded.
- **dataType** - The data type expected of the server response.
- **data** - Specifies data to be sent to the server.
- **success(result,status,xhr)** - A function to run when the request succeeds.
- **error(xhr,status,error)** - A function to run when the request fails.

Chapter 8 - Puzzles

Puzzles, riddles, logical questions, and lateral thinking questions are an important part of the selection process for many job interviewers.

They are usually fun. In the context of being interviewed, however, they can be a very stressful exercise.

Keep in mind that when being challenged with a complicated puzzle to solve, hiring managers don't require candidates to score well. What is important when recruiting is to assess the interviewees' ability to reason logically, and determine their ability to think out of the box.

It is beneficial to walk through your thought process out loud, even if not asked, so that the interviewer understand the way you process the information given, and how you get to a solution.

This chapter provides typical puzzle and logical questions asked during technical interviews, along with their solution.

Mathematical

Ant and Triangle Problem

Three ants are sitting at the three corners of an equilateral triangle. Each ant starts with a randomly picked direction and starts to move along the edge of the triangle.

What is the probability that none of the ants collide?

Ant and Triangle Solution

The ants can only avoid a collision if they all decide to move in the same direction (either clockwise or anti-clockwise). Because, if the ants do not pick the same direction, there will definitely be a collision.

Each ant has the option to either move clockwise or anti-clockwise. There is a one in two chance that an ant decides to pick a particular direction.

So, we have:

- Total combination = 2 x 2 x 2 (as for each ant there are 2 choices)
- Total favourable directions = 2 (either all clockwise, or all anti-clockwise)

Hence the solution: **P** = 2/8 = 1/4 = **0.25**

100 Doors Puzzle

This puzzling has been asked at major tech companies: Google, Adobe, Amazon and Oracle.

There are 100 doors in a row, all doors are initially closed. A person walks through all doors multiple times and toggle (if it's open then close, if closed then open) them in following way:

- In first walk, the person toggles every door
- In second walk, the person toggles every second door, i.e: 2nd, 4th, 6th, 8th, ...
- In third walk, the person toggles every third door, i.e: 3rd, 6th, 9th, ...

What state are the doors after the last pass?
Which are open which are closed?

100 Doors Solution

You can figure that for any given door, say door #38, you will visit it for every divisor it has.
that would be 1 & 38, 2 & 19. So, on pass 1, I will open the door; on pass 2, I will close it, on pass 19 open, on pass 38 close.

For every pair of divisors the door will just end up back in its initial state. You might think that every door will end up closed? Well what about door #9? Door 9 has the divisors 1 & 9, 3 & 3. but 3 is repeated because 9 is a perfect square, so you will only visit door #9, on pass 1, 3, and 9... leaving it open at the end. Only perfect square doors will be open at the end.

So the answer is that the open doors, after all passes, are: 1, 4, 9, 16, 25, 36, 49, 64, 81 and 100.

Logical

Crossing the Bridge problem

Four people need to cross a rickety bridge at night. Unfortunately, they only have **one** torch and the bridge is too dangerous to cross without it.

The bridge is only strong enough to support two people at a time, and not all people take the same time to cross the bridge. Times for each person:

- 01 min
- 02 mins
- 07 mins
- 10 mins

What is the shortest time needed for all four of them to cross the bridge?

Crossing the Bridge Solution

It is **17 mins**

1 and 2 go first, then 1 comes back.
Then 7 and 10 go and 2 comes back. Then 1 and 2 go again, it makes a total of 17 minutes.

Apple and Oranges

There are three boxes. One is labeled *Apples* another is labeled *Oranges*. The last one is labeled *Apples and Oranges*. You know that each box is labeled incorrectly. You may ask me to pick one fruit from one box.

Which do you choose to be able to then label all boxes correctly?

Apple and Oranges Solution

Pick from the one labeled *Apples and Oranges*. This box must contain either only apples or only oranges.

E.g: If you find an Orange, label the box *Oranges*, then change the *Oranges* box to *Apples,* and the *Apples* box to *Apples and Oranges*.

Heaven or Hell

You are standing before two doors. One of the path leads to heaven and the other one leads to hell. There are two guardians, one by each door. You know one of them always tells the truth and the other always lies, but you don't know who is the honest one and who is the liar.

You can only ask one question to one of them in order to find the way to heaven. What is the question?

Heaven or Hell Solution

The question you should ask is *If I ask the other guard about which side leads to heaven, what would he answer?*.

It should be fairly easy to see that irrespective of whom do you ask this question, you will always get an answer which leads to hell. So you can chose the other path to continue your journey to heaven.

This idea was famously used in the 1986 film *Labyrinth*. Here is further explanation and thought process.

Let us assume that the left door leads to heaven.

If you ask the guard which speaks truth about which path leads to heaven, as he speaks always the truth, he would say *left*. Now the liar, when he is asked what the other guard (truth teller) would answer, he would definitely say *right*.

Similarly, if you ask the liar about which path leads to heaven, he would say *right*. As the truth teller speaks nothing but the truth, he would say *right* when he is asked what the other guard (liar) would answer. So in any case, you would end up having the path to hell as an answer. So you can chose the other path as a way to heaven.

10 Coins Puzzles

You are blindfolded and 10 coins are placed in front of you on the table. You are allowed to touch the coins, but can't tell whether tail or head is up. You are told that there are 5 coins head up, and 5 coins tails up but not which ones are which.

How do you make two piles of coins each with the same number of heads up? You can flip the coins any number of times.

10 Coins Solution

Make 2 piles with equal number of coins. Then, simply flip all the coins from 1 of the piles.

Explanation via example:

We know there are 5 heads, suppose we divide all 10 coins in 2 piles.

Case:

- **P1**: H H T T T
- **P2**: H H H T T

Now when P1 is flipped, we get:

- **P1**: T T H H H

P1(T T H H H) = P2(H H H T T)
Another case:

- **P1**: H T T T T
- **P2**: H H H H T

When P1 will be flipped, we get:

- **P1**: H H H H T

P1(H T T T T) = P2(H H H H T)

Explanation via abstracted reasoning

Since the requested number of each type of coin is 5H one pile and 5T on the other, whenever we make two piles (P1 and P2) of equal coins, this always true outcome can be deducted:

- Given that P1 has x heads, then P2 has 5 minus x heads
- Given than P1 has y tails, then P2 has 5 minus y tails
- Given that P2 has x heads, then P1 has 5 minus x heads
- Given than P2 has y tails, then P1 has 5 minus y tails

So flipping one pile will result in the same number H and T coins.

How Old Are My Children?

Two old friends, Jack and Bill, meet after a long time.

Jack: *Hey, how are you man?*
Bill: *Not bad, got married and I have three kids now.*
Jack: *That's awesome. How old are they?*
Bill: *The product of their ages is 72 and the sum of their ages is the same as your birth day of the month.*
Jack: *Cool... But I still don't know.*
Bill: *My oldest kid just started taking piano lessons.*
Jack: *Oh now I get it.*

How old are Bill's kids?

How Old Are My Children Solution

Let's break it down. The product of their ages is 72. So what are the possible choices?

1. 2, 2, 18: sum(2, 2, 18) = 22
2. 2, 4, 9: sum(2, 4, 9) = 15
3. 2, 6, 6: sum(2, 6, 6) = 14
4. 2, 3, 12: sum(2, 3, 12) = 17
5. 3, 4, 6: sum(3, 4, 6) = 13
6. 3, 3, 8: sum(3, 3, 8) = 14
7. 1, 8, 9: sum(1,8,9) = 18
8. 1, 3, 24: sum(1, 3, 24) = 28
9. 1, 4, 18: sum(1, 4, 18) = 23
10. 1, 2, 36: sum(1, 2, 36) = 39
11. 1, 6, 12: sum(1, 6, 12) = 19

We have 11 possibilities, but we also know that:

The sum of their ages is the same as Jack's birth date. That could be anything from 1 to 31 but Jack, who certainly know his own birthday was unable to find out the ages, it means there are two or more combinations with the same sum. From the choices above, only two of them are possible now:

1. 2, 6, 6 – sum(2, 6, 6) = 14
2. 3, 3, 8 – sum(3, 3, 8) = 14

We still have 2 possibilities, Bill then gave Jack the last clue, he has an **oldest** kid, hence only one, who has started taking piano lessons.

We can eliminate combination 1 since there would be two eldest ones. The answer is **3, 3 and 8**.

Out of the Box thinking

3 Switches 1 Bulb

There are 3 switches in a room, all off. One of them turns on a bulb in the room next door. You can not see whether the bulb is on or off, until you enter the room.

What is the **minimum** number of times you need to go into the room to determine which switch turns on the bulb?

3 Switches 1 Bulb Solution

The answer just is **one time**. I only have to go to that room once.

1. Switch ON the first switch, keep it on for say 2-3 minutes
2. Switch OFF the first switch then switch ON the second switch
3. As soon as the second switch is ON, I go to the room.

If I find that the bulb is glowing, that means the second switch connects to the bulb. If not, then I touch the bulb, if it is warm that means it corresponds to the first switch, if not then it corresponds to the third switch.

Burning Rope Timer

A man has two ropes of varying thickness.
Those two ropes are not identical, they are not the same density nor the same length, nor the same width.
Each rope burns in exactly 60 minutes.

The man wants to measure 45 mins. How can he measure 45 mins using only these two ropes and a lighter.

Note: Half a rope wouln't burn in 30 mins, because it's non-homogeneous.

Burning Rope Timer Solution

He can burn one of the rope from both its ends and the second rope at one end.

After half an hour, the first one burns completely and at this point of time, he will burn the other end of the second rope so now it will take 15 mins more to completely burn.

So that total time of 45 mins (30 mins + 15 mins) can be measured.

Half the Cake

Consider a rectangular cake with a rectangular section (of any size or orientation removed from it). Is it possible to divide the cake exactly in half with only one cut?

Half the Cake Solution

It's a relatively easy problem to solve but many logical people might over think the situation, by asking further information about the rectangular section, its position in particular.

The right answer is **yes** it is possible, by slicing it sideways (depth cut)

Egg fall

This puzzle requiring outside of the box thinking, because the common logical reasoning applied sadly does not provide the right answer.

You have two identical eggs. Standing in front of a 100 floor building, you wonder what is the maximum number of floors from which the egg can be dropped without breaking it.

What is the minimum number of tries needed to find out the solution?

Egg fall Solution

The easiest way, dumb approach, to do this would be to start from the first floor and drop the egg. If it doesn't break, move on to the next floor. If it does break, then we know the maximum floor the egg will survive is 0. If we continue this process, we will easily find out the maximum floors the egg will survive with just one egg. So the maximum number of tries is 100 that is when the egg survives even at the 100th floor.

Can we do better? Of course we can. Let's start at the second floor. If the egg breaks, then we can use the second egg to go back to the first floor and try again. If it does not break, then we can go ahead and try on the 4th floor (in multiples of 2). If it ever breaks, say at floor x, then we know it survived floor x-2. That leaves us with just floor x-1 to try with the second egg. So what is the maximum number of tries possible? It occurs when the egg survives 98 or 99 floors. It will take 50 tries to reach floor 100 and one more egg to try on the 99th floor so the total is 51 tries. Wow, that is almost half of what we had last time.

Can we do even better? Yes we can. What if we try at intervals of 3? Applying the same logic as the previous case, we need a max of 35 tries to find out the information (33 tries to reach 99th floor and 2 more on 97th and 98th floor).

What about intervals of 4, or 5? The table below with trials would show the optimal max attempt to be 19 attempts. with intervals of 8, 9, 10, 11, 12, or 13.

Number of intervals, along with attempts needed:

1. – 100 attempts
2. – 51 attempts
3. – 35 attempts
4. – 29 attempts
5. – 25 attempts
6. – 21 attempts
7. – 20 attempts
8. – 19 attempts
9. – 19 attempts
10. – 19 attempts
11. – 19 attempts
12. – 19 attempts
13. – 19 attempts
14. – 20 attempts
15. – 20 attempts
16. – 21 attempts

So picking any one of the intervals with 19 maximum tries would be supposedly the most optimal approach.

Egg fall Best solution

Instead of taking equal intervals, we can increase the number of floors by one less than the previous increment.

For example, let's first try at floor 14. If it breaks, then we need 13 more tries to find the solution. If it doesn't break, then we should try floor 27 (14 + 13). If it breaks, we need 12 more tries to find the solution.

So the initial 2 tries plus the additional 12 tries would still be 14 tries in total. If it doesn't break, we can try 39 (27 + 12) and so on. Using 14 as the initial floor, we can reach up to floor 105 (14 + 13 + 12 + ... + 1) before we need more than 14 tries. Since we only need to cover 100 floors, 14 tries is sufficient to find the solution.

Therefore, **14 is the least number of tries**

The King and the poisoned wine

This puzzle has been asked during interviews for software development roles at Microsoft.

A King is about to have his 50th birthday celebration. The celebration is in 24 hours and is the most important party he has ever hosted. He has 1000 bottles of wine he was planning to open for the celebration, but he just found out that one of them is poisoned.

He doesn't know which one, but while poison it contains is very lethal it doesn't exhibits no symptoms until death. Death occurs within ten to twenty hours after consuming even the minutest amount of poison. He has over a thousand slaves at his disposal and just under 24 hours to determine which single bottle is poisoned.

Among those slaves, a handful of prisoners are about to be executed, and it would shame the King to have anyone else killed.

What is the smallest number of people the King must have to drink from the bottles to be absolutely sure to find the poisoned bottle within 24 hours?

The King and the poisoned wine Solution

The answer lies in conversion of integers to binary form.

Label each bottle using binary digits. Assign each prisoner to one of the binary flags. Prisoners must take a sip from each bottle where their binary flag is set.

With **ten prisoners**, there are 1024 unique combinations so we can test up to 1024 bottles of wine.

Each of the ten prisoners will take a quick small sip from about 500 bottles. Small sips not only leave more wine for guests. Small sips also avoid death by alcohol poisoning. As long as each prisoner is administered about a millilitre from each bottle, they will only consume the equivalent of about one bottle of wine each.

Bonus saving 2 prisoners

Each prisoner will have at least a fifty percent chance of living. There is only one binary combination where all prisoners must sip from the wine. If there are ten prisoners then there are ten more combinations where all but one prisoner must sip from the wine. By avoiding these two types of combinations you can ensure no more than **8 prisoners** die.

Although the solution just involves binary form representation of integers, it requires an out of the box thinking to solve it.

PART II - Non Technical

This part covers non technical aspects of job interviews. We will discuss how to create a great resume and cover letter, also present common interview formats to be expected when applying for a technical job.

Often overlooked is the fact that soft skills, such as communication, business acumen, creativity and impact your work has had in the past is as important as your coding and problem solving skills.

Chapter 9 - Resume

This chapter will cover How your resume is screened and provide you with 10 Ways To Improve Your Resume

How Your Resume is Screened

While many engineers might be qualified for the role they are applying for, they miss out on getting a shot at the interview if never get past resume screening. The main issue when you don't understand how recruiters work.

Before writing your resume, it is important to understand the recruiting structure and how recruiting is done.

The Skill Set Checklist

Before starting the search for candidates, I usually consult very closely with the team and the hiring manager to find out the specific skill sets that are relevant for the position. These skill sets are typically grouped into *Must have, Good to have*, and *Special bonus*.

- **Must have**—Typically, most of the must-haves include a college degree in the relevant technical field, and perhaps a few years of experience in a particular programming language or technology.
- **Good to have**—Includes experience and familiarity with secondary languages/technologies which may not be directly relevant to what the candidate would be working on, but could be required due to some interfacing with other components of the project. It could also include softer skills such as being a team player, clear communication, etc.

- **Special bonus**—Recognized skill sets and experiences that are difficult to come by. Probably not a requirement, but would definitely be useful for the position.

Now that I am armed with this list, the search for candidates begin.

Typically, I do not seek that "one perfect candidate". What I seek for is the "best fit candidate". The search is essentially a numbers game. I know that for a specific job posting, there will be a number of X applicants. At each stage of the interview process, some percentage of the candidates will be eliminated, leaving only a final Y% of the initial pool to choose from. Since Y tends to be a rather small number, recruiters will try to maximize X.

The 10 Seconds Glance

When I am looking at a resume, I am doing a keyword match against the skill set checklist. If I see a good amount of the right keywords in the resume, it is a pass. If I need to spend more than 10 seconds trying to figure out what's in there, it is a fail. If I see an excessive amount of keywords (much looking like spam), it signals a red flag and goes into the "maybe". Depending on whether I think I have enough candidates for the day, you could eventually go into the pass or fail stack.

There are lots of articles writing about how recruiters only spend an average of about 10 seconds to screen each resume. The news is, this is true because resume screening is such a menial, robotic and repetitive task. In fact, many applicant tracking systems (ATS) now are so advanced that they can parse your resume automatically, search for specific keywords in your resume, and score your resume based on the weights pre-assigned to each keyword.

Finding a job is a two-way fit. The company wants someone with the relevant skills, but it is also important for the applicant to fit in the company culture, and be able to gain something out of his stint. Hence, honesty is the single most important criteria in a resume.

There is a delicate balance between finding the right job vs. finding a job. Getting rejected does not always mean you are not good enough. Sometimes, it just means you are not a right fit for what the company is looking for.

When hiring fresh grads, I know that many of them will not have as much experience as someone who has years of industry practice. Hence, I would look out more for soft skills, such as attention to detail, initiative, passion, ability to get things done, etc.

10 Ways To Improve Your Resume

Now that you are aware of how recruiters screen your resume, here are 10 actionable ways you can do to improve it.

1. Cover letter

- A short introduction describing who you are and what you're looking for.
- What projects have you enjoyed working on?
- What motivates you?
- Links to to your online profiles (GitHub, Twitter, LinkedIn etc.).

- A description of your work history (whether as a resume, or prose).

I've often received resumes with no cover letters, and I am perfectly fine with it. If you ask me, it is better to have no cover letter than to have a bad cover letter, especially if your cover letter is a "templated" content. An effective cover letter needs to highlight the fit between the job requirements and your skills/experiences. Do not just tell what you have done in your cover letter; explain how it is a fit for what the company is looking for.

Some small nitpicks:

- Make sure, if possible, that the cover letter is addressed to the right person (either the name of the recruiter if it is known, or to a generic hiring manager) and company.
- Run a spell check.

2. Length of resume

Your resume should be kept to 1 page or a **maximum** of 2 pages. Include only your most recent and relevant experiences.

Information that a recruiter wants to know:

- Name, email, contact number.
- Education details: College, Major, GPA, academic awards, availability.
- If you have studied abroad, you can list that too.
- Projects that you have worked on.
- Work experience/co-curricular activities.
- Non profit contributions.
- Skills/other interests.

- Street cred - GitHub/StackOverflow/LinkedIn profile (optional, but highly recommended).

Information nobody needs to know:

- Your profile picture.
- Address, home phone number, gender, religion, race, marital status, etc.
- Elementary, middle, high school.
- Your low GPA.
- Anything about your parents/siblings, their names, occupation, etc.
- Your life story.
- Anything not relevant to the job you are applying for (e.g. that you have a driving license when you are applying to be a programmer).

Ideally, keep it short, concise, but provide details you believe are relevant.

3. GPA does matter

Everyone wants the cream of the crop. In the absence of a standardized test, GPA serves as that indicator. While GPA may not necessarily be a good indication of how well you can code, a high GPA would definitely put you in a more favorable position to the recruiter.

If your GPA is rather low, but you have loads of technical experiences, you can try not listing your GPA in the resume. This kinda "forces" the recruiter to read through your projects/job experience, and perhaps grant you a first interview. If you manage to impress them, who cares about your GPA? But if your GPA is low and you do not have skills for the job... maybe you should work on one of them and revisit job applications later.

Some students have low GPA, but it might be due to some irrelevant classes which they did badly in. E.g. Student X is scoring A for all his programming classes, but did not do well for his language classes. If I am hiring a developer, Student X would still be a suitable candidate despite his low GPA. In such cases, it might even be recommended to attach a transcript along with the resume.

Also, when you list your GPA/results, try to benchmark it. Instead of simply listing 4.6, write 4.6/5.0 (First Class Honors or Summa Cum Laude). To the recruiter, 4.6 does not mean anything if he/she is not familiar with your grading system.

4. Be clear about your objectives

Are you looking for a summer internship/full-time employment? What position are you applying for? Read the job description and **know the job you are applying for**.

"Work experience" does not mean any work experience; it means **relevant work experience**. If you are applying for a developer position, the recruiter is not interested to know that you were a student escort for girls walking back to their apartments at night, nor that you were a cashier at Starbucks. You would be better off writing about the project you did for some programming class - yes, even if it was just a school project. Tailor your experiences and projects according to the job you are applying for. Pick relevant details to emphasize on and do not be hesitant to drop stuff completely if they are totally irrelevant. Quality over quantity.

- Make sure the description is comprehensive. Avoid writing "Software engineering intern - write code".

You are better off not writing anything.

- Based on my experience, most fresh grads do not have extremely relevant job experience (unless you are lucky to have scored a really rewarding internship). For developer positions, I think it is ok to not have any job experience and just personal projects.

5. Reverse chronological order

Always list your resume in reverse chronological order - the most recent at the top. Recruiters are more interested in what you have worked on recently than what you worked on 3 years ago. Chances are, you probably forgot the details too anyway.

6. Make sure you are contactable

- Get a proper email account with ideally your first name and last name, eg. *john.doe@gmail.com* instead of *angrybirds88@gmail.com*.
- If you are using your school's .edu email, try to have an alias like *john.doe@xxx.edu* instead of *a002342342@xxx.edu*.
- Avoid emails like *me@christi.na* or *admin@[mycooldomain].com* -- because it's prone to typo errors.
- Make sure the number you have listed is the best way to reach you. The last thing you want is to miss a call from the recruiter because you typed the wrong number, or you are not available on that number during office hours (most probably the times the recruiter will call).

7. Layout/Formatting/Design

- Be consistent with the way you format your resume. Italics, underline, bold, and how they are used.
- Keep it simple with single standard font, avoid fancy fonts like Comic Sans and do not have too many varying styles/font sizes/color.
- Be consistent about the way you list your dates (eg. May 2011 - Aug 2011). Avoid using numerals for both month and date due to the difference in style for MMDD and DDMM in different countries. Dates like "Aug 2011 - June 12" just show that you have zero attention to detail.
- Unless you are applying for a design job, just stick to the standard "table" style for the resume. It helps the recruiter screen your resume more efficiently since they are trained through experience to read that format. It would also help in the automatic scoring by the ATS. The last thing you want is for your application to be rejected because the system could not parse your resume for it to be scored. That being said, I am not discouraging you from coming up with your own design. It is nice to read something different. Just be aware of the risks you are taking.
- Name your file firstname_lastname_resume.pdf instead of resume.pdf - it is easier for recruiters to search/forward.
- PDF is preferred over Word doc.
- Be consistent with your bullet points.
- Your resume should not look sparse. If you really have trouble filling it up, you are either not thinking hard enough, or not doing enough. In the case of the latter, consider working on your personal projects (i.e. stuff you can post on GitHub). That being said, do not write stuff just to fill space.
- This should be common sense, but do not commit fraud, i.e. apply for the same job using a different name, or using your friend's resume to apply for the same job. Some ATS issues an indicator if they suspect the application to be a duplicate.

- Try to keep white space down to a minimum. This will also help reduce the length of your resume to one page. Reduce margins and paddings reasonably.
- Show your resume to friends and relative for feedback on its layout.

8. Listing Your skills

It is useful to list your relevant skills in a quick summary section for easy reading/matching. However, many people make the mistake of listing as many skills/programming languages in the resume as possible. This may get you through the ATS scoring, but it definitely would not leave a good impression on the recruiter - the actual human reading your resume and deciding whether to call you up for an interview!

Ideally, if your resume is good enough, the recruiter should already know what you are proficient in. The skills section is just a quick summary/reiteration. Listing a bunch of technologies you claim you know without actually showing how you have worked with them is suspect.

9. Projects

- Ideally, 1-2 lines about the project, 2-3 lines about your role, what technologies you used, what you did, your learning, etc. These can be Final Year Projects, Research projects, projects for a particular class, freelance projects, or just personal projects (ie. GitHub stuff).
- Ideally, 2 to 3 projects that align with your interests/position you are applying for.
- You want the project section to demonstrate your personality and skills, and be the talking point during the interview.

10. Online profile/other interests

Here's the news - Recruiters do search for your name! Definitely pre-empt that by Googling/Facebooking/searching yourself on all forms of social media to see what turns up. Make sure your privacy settings are restricted so your online profile shows only the image you are trying to project.

If you have some space on your resume, it is good to list additional interests outside of coding. Eg. skiing, water sports, soccer, etc etc. Gives the interviewer something to talk to you about. It also shows that you are a well-rounded individual/cool person to hang out with.

References

- Screening your resume is like playing word search
- 10 tips to get past resume screening for College Students/Grads

Chapter 10 - Interview Formats

The following interview formats are based on reported experiences interviewing with companies in the Bay Area. Formats would differ slightly depending on the roles you are applying to. Many companies like to use CoderPad for collaborative code editing. CoderPad supports running of the program, so you might be asked to fix your code such that it can be run. For front end interviews, many companies like to use CodePen, and it will be worth your time to familiarize yourself with the user interfaces of those web-based coding environments.

For on-site interviews at smaller (non-public) companies, many will allow or even ask that you use your own laptop. Hence it is important that you prepare your development environment in advance.

Airbnb

- Recruiter phone screen.
- Technical phone interview:
    - 1 or 2 x Algorithm/front end on CoderPad/CodePen.
- On-site (General):
    - 2 x Algorithm coding on CoderPad.
    - 1 x System design/architecture.
    - 1 x Past experience/project.
    - 2 x Cross functional.
- On-site (Front End):
    - 2 x Front end coding on CodePen. Use any framework/library.
    - 1 x General coding on your own laptop.
    - 1 x Past experience/project.
    - 2 x Cross functional.

Tips

- All sessions involve coding on your own laptop. Prepare your development environment in advance.
- You are allowed to look up APIs if you need to.
- They seem to place high emphasis on compilable, runnable code in all their coding rounds.
- Cross functional interviews will involve getting Airbnb employees from any discipline to speak with you. These interviews are mostly non-technical but are extremely important to Airbnb because they place a high emphasis on cultural fit.

Asana

- Recruiter phone screen.
- Technical phone interview.
- On-site (Product Engineer):
  - 3 x Algorithm and system design on whiteboard within the same session.
  - 1 x Algorithm on laptop and system design. This session involves writing code on your own laptop to solve 3 well-defined algorithm problems in around 45 minutes after which an engineer will come in and review the code with you. You are not supposed to run the code while working on the problem.
- Tips:
  - No front end questions were asked.
  - Asana places high emphasis on System Design and makes heavy use of the whiteboard. You do not necessarily have to write code for the algorithm question of the first three interviews.
  - All 4 sessions involve algorithms and system design. One of the sessions will be conducted by an Engineering Manager.

- The last session will involve coding on your own laptop. Prepare your development environment in advance.
- Regardless of Product Engineer or Engineering Generalist position, their interview format and questions are similar.

Dropbox

- Recruiter phone screen.
- Technical phone interviews:
  - 2 x Algorithm/front end on CoderPad/CodePen.
- On-site (Front End):
  - 2 x Front end on CodePen. Only Vanilla JS or jQuery allowed.
  - 1 x General coding on CoderPad.
  - 1 x All around. Meet with an Engineering Manager and discussing past experiences and working style.

Tips

- You can code on your own laptop and look up APIs.
- Dropbox recruiters are very nice and will give you helpful information on what kind of questions to expect for the upcoming sessions.
- One of the front end sessions involve coding up a pixel-perfect version of a real page on www.dropbox.com. You'll be given a spec of the desired page and you'll be asked to create a working version during the interview.

Facebook

- Recruiter phone screen.
- Technical phone interviews:

- o 1 or 2 x Algorithm/front end on Skype/CoderPad.
- On-site (Front End):
  - o 2 x Technical coding interview on whiteboard (Ninja).
  - o 1 x Behavioural (Jedi). Meet with an Engineering Manager and discussing past experiences and working style.
  - o 1 x Design/architecture on whiteboard (Pirate).

Tips

- You are only allowed to use the whiteboard (or wall). No laptops involved.
- For the Jedi round, you may be asked a technical question at the end of it. Front end candidates will be given a small HTML/CSS problem nearing the end of the session.
- For the Ninja rounds, you may be asked one to two questions depending on how fast you progress through the question.

Google

- Recruiter phone screen.
- Technical phone interview:
  - o 1 or 2 x algorithm on Google Doc.
- On-site (Front End):
  - o 3 x Front end on whiteboard. Have to use Vanilla JS (or at the most, jQuery).
  - o 2 x Algorithm on whiteboard.
- Team matching.
  - o Speak with managers from different teams who are interested in your profile.

Tips

- You are only allowed to use the whiteboard. No laptops involved.
- In rare cases, candidates may even be allowed to skip the phone interview round and advanced to on-site directly.
- For non-fresh grads, you only receive an offer if you are successfully matched with a team.

Lyft

- Recruiter phone screen.
- Technical phone interview:
    - 1 x Algorithm/Front end over JSFiddle.
- On-site (Front End):
    - 4 x Front end on Coderpad/your own laptop. Use any language/framework.
    - 1 x Behavioural. Meet with an Engineering Manager and go through candidate's resume.

Tips

- Can use whiteboard and/or laptop.
- For front end coding, I opted to use React and had to set up the projects on the spot using create-react-app.

Palantir

- Recruiter phone screen.
- Technical phone interview:
    - 1 x Algorithm over HackerRank CodePair and Skype.
- On-site (General):
    - 2 x Algorithm on whiteboard.
    - 1 x Decomposition (system design) on whiteboard.
- On-site (Front End):

- 1 x Front end on your own laptop. This session lasts about 1.5 hours. Use any library/framework.
- 1 x Decomposition (system design) on whiteboard.

Tips

- I opted to use React and had to set up projects on the spot using create-react-app.
- You may be asked to meet with Engineering Managers after the technical sessions and it's not necessarily a good/bad thing.

WhatsApp

- Recruiter phone screen.
- Technical phone interview:
    - 2 x Algorithm over CoderPad.
- On-site (Web Client Developer):
    - 4 x Algorithm on whiteboard.

Tips

- No front end questions were asked.
- 1 of the interviewers is an Engineering Manager.

Chapter 11 - The Interview

The Elevator Pitch

The Elevator Pitch is very efficient tool to move forward in your career. An Elevator Pitch an approach to pitch yourself to an executive that you want to impress. Whether you're at a job event with many other candidates and you have a short opportunity time to explain who you are to a connection or client, it is important to be able to clearly describe your knowledge and skillset quickly and succinctly. Here are some tips to develop a good Elevator Pitch:

1. Sell yourself. The whole point is to get you a job or make a connection that benefits your career. Tell them who you are, who you work for, or study, and what you do.
2. KISS (Keep It Simple, Stupid). Tell them some highlights from your most impressive projects. Do not delve into the depths of how you reverse engineered a game or decrypted a TCP/IP packet for prediction. Tell them the executive summary: "I reverse engineered X game by decrypting Y packet to predict Z." If this catches their interest, they *will* ask further questions on their own.
3. Why do *they* want *you*? This is where you use your knowledge of the company, knowledge of their technology stack, your unique talent that they want, etc. in order to solidify your ability to contribute to their company.
4. PRACTICE! Lastly, you must practice your pitch. Having a great, succinct summary of your skills only helps if you can actually deliver it rapidly and with confidence. You should practice keeping a quick but easy-to-follow pace that won't overwhelm them but

won't bore them. It's a precarious balance, but can be ironed out with practice.

Having an Elevator Pitch at hand is a great way to create a network and happen upon new job opportunities. There will often be times when you can't prepare for an interview or meeting, and it is incredibly useful to have a practiced pitch.

References

- The Elevator Pitch

10 Psychological Tricks

Here are some psychological tricks that will help you ace a job interview.

1. Tailor your answers to the interviewer's age.

- Generation Y interviewers (between 20 and 30): Bring along visual samples of your work and highlight your ability to multitask.
- Generation X interviewers (between 30 and 50): Emphasize your creativity and mention how work/life balance contributes to your success.
- Baby Boomer interviewers (between 50 and 70): Show that you work hard and demonstrate respect for what they've achieved.

2. Hold your palms open or steeple your hands.
3. Find something in common with your interviewer.
4. Mirror the interviewer's body language.
5. Compliment the interviewer and the organization without self-promoting. Specifically, the students who ingratiated themselves praised the organization and indicated their enthusiasm for working there, and complimented the interviewer. They didn't play

up the value of positive events they took credit for or take credit for positive events even if they weren't solely responsible.

6. Show confidence and deference simultaneously. In a job interview, that means showing deference to your interviewer, while also demonstrating self-confidence. One way to do that is to say something like, "I love your work on [whatever area]. It reminds me of my work on [whatever area]."

7. Emphasize how you took control of events in your previous jobs. To impress your interviewer, you should talk about past work experiences where you took initiative.

8. Be candid about your weaknesses. It's wiser to say something genuine like, "I'm not always the best at staying organized," which sounds more honest, and could make your interviewer more inclined to recommend you for the position.

9. Think of the interview as a conversation. While it may be difficult to do, don't think of it as a job interview. Think of it as a conversation between two people who are trying to get to know one another and to see if they will be compatible working together. Also, keep in mind that the hiring manager may be nervous, too, so if you walk in with a smile, you can put them at ease which will help put you at ease.

10. Showcase your potential. You might be tempted to tell your interviewer all about your past accomplishments — but research suggests you should focus more on what you could do in the future, if that organization hires you.

References

- Business Insider

Interview Questions By Companies

Learn the <u>STAR</u> format.

- **Situation** - The interviewer wants you to present a recent challenge and situation in which you found yourself.
- **Task** - What were you required to achieve? The interviewer will be looking to see what you were trying to achieve from the situation. Some performance development methods use "Target" rather than "Task". Job interview candidates who describe a "Target" they set themselves instead of an externally imposed "Task" emphasize their own intrinsic motivation to perform and to develop their performance.
- **Action** - What did you do? The interviewer will be looking for information on what you did, why you did it and what the alternatives were.
- **Results** - What was the outcome of your actions? What did you achieve through your actions and did you meet your objectives? What did you learn from this experience and have you used this learning since?

General

- Why do you want to work for X company?
- Why do you want to leave your current/last company?
- What are you looking for in your next role?
- Tell me about a time when you had a conflict with a co-worker.
- Tell me about a time in which you had a conflict and needed to influence somebody else.
- What project are you currently working on?
- What is the most challenging aspect of your current project?
- What was the most difficult bug that you fixed in the past 6 months?

- How do you tackle challenges? Name a difficult challenge you faced while working on a project, how you overcame it, and what you learned.
- What are you excited about?
- What frustrates you?
- Imagine it is your first day here at the company. What do you want to work on? What features would you improve on?
- What are the most interesting projects you have worked on and how might they be relevant to this company's environment?
- Tell me about a time you had a disagreement with your manager.
- Talk about a project you are most passionate about, or one where you did your best work.
- What does your best day of work look like?
- What is something that you had to push for in your previous projects?
- What is the most constructive feedback you have received in your career?
- What is something you had to persevere at for multiple months?

Airbnb

Source: Glassdoor

While loving to travel or appreciating Airbnb's growth may be good answers, try to demonstrate the deep connection you have with the product.

- What does "belong anywhere" mean to you?
- What large problems in the world would you solve today?
- Why do you like Airbnb?
- If you had an unlimited budget and you could buy one gift for one person, what would you buy and who would you buy it for?

- If you had an unlimited budget and you could go somewhere, where would you go?
- Share one of your trips with us.
- What is the most challenging project in or out of school that you have worked on in the last 6 months.
- What is something that you don't want from your last internship/job?
- Give me an example of when you've been a good host.
- What's something you'd like to remove from the Airbnb experience?
- What is something new that you can teach your interviewer in a few minutes?
- Tell me about why you want to work here.
- What is the best gift you have ever given or received?
- Tell me about a time you were uncomfortable and how you dealt with it.
- Explain a project that you worked on recently.
- What do you think of Airbnb?
- Tell me something about yourself and why you'd be a good fit for the position.
- Name a situation where you were impressed by a company's customer service.
- How did you work with senior management on large projects as well as multiple internal teams?
- Tell me about a time you had to give someone terrible news.
- What excites you about the company?
- How does Airbnb impact our guests and hosts?
- What part of our mission resonates the most with you?

Amazon

Source: Glassdoor

- How do you deal with a failed deadline?
- Why do you want to work for Amazon?

- Tell me about a situation where you had a conflict with a teammate.
- In my professional experience have you worked on something without getting approval from your manager?
- Tell me a situation where you would have done something differently from what you actually did.
- What is the most exceedingly bad misstep you've made at any point?
- Describe what Human Resources means to you.
- How would you improve Amazon's website?

Dropbox

Source: Glassdoor

- Talk about your favorite project.
- If you were hired here what would you do?
- State an experience about how you solved a technical problem. Be specific about the diagnosis and process.

Hired

Source: Glassdoor

- Tell me about yourself.
- What is your biggest strength and area of growth?
- Why are you interested in this opportunity?
- What are your salary expectations?
- Why are you looking to leave your current company?
- Tell me about a time your work responsibilities got a little overwhelming. What did you do?
- Give me an example of a time when you had a difference of opinion with a team member. How did you handle that?
- Tell me about a challenge you faced recently in your role. How did you tackle it? What was the outcome?

- Where do you want to be in five years?
- Tell me about a time you needed information from someone who wasn't responsive. What did you do?

Lyft

Source: <u>Glassdoor</u>

- Tell me about your most interesting/challenging project to date.
- Why Lyft? What are you looking for in the next role?

Palantir

Source: <u>Glassdoor</u>

- How do you deal with difficult coworkers? Think about specific instances where you resolved conflicts.
- How did you win over the difficult employees?
- Tell me about an analytical problem that you have worked on in the past.
- What are your three strengths and three weaknesses?
- If you were in charge of picking projects for Palantir, what problem would you try to solve?
- **What is something 90% of people disagree with you about?**
- What are some of the best and worst things about your current company?
- **What is broken around you?**
- What would your manager say about you?
- Describe Palantir to your grandmother.
- Teach me something you've learned.
- Tell me a time when you predicted something.
- If your supervisors were to rate you on a scale of 1-10, what would they rate you?
- What was the most fun thing you did recently?

- Tell me the story of how you became who you are today and what made you apply to Palantir.

Slack

Source: Glassdoor

- Tell me something about your internship.
- Why do you want to join Slack?
- Tell me about your past projects.
- Explain me your toughest project and the working architecture.
- Apart from technical knowledge, what did you learn during your internship?
- If someone has a different viewpoint to do a project like different programming language, how would handle this situation?
- What are your most interesting subjects and why?
- Did you find any bugs in Slack?
- What is your favorite feature and why?

Stack Overflow

Source: Glassdoor

- What have you built?
- What is the hardest technical problem you have run into?
- How did you solve it?
- Where do you see yourself in 5 years?
- Why do you want to work here?
- How do you handle disagreements with coworkers?

Stripe

Source: Glassdoor

- How do you stay up to date with the latest technologies?
- Explain a project that you worked on recently that was difficult.
- Where do you see yourself in five years?

Chapter 12 - Questions to Ask

Here are some good questions to ask at the end of the interview, extracted from various sources. The ones in **bold** are the ones that tend to make the interviewer go "That's a good question" and pause and think for a bit.

General

- **What are you most proud about in your career so far?**
- **What is the most important/valuable thing you have learnt from working here?**
- How do your clients and customers define success?
- What would you change around here if you could?
- What are some weaknesses of the organization?
- What does a typical day look like for you?
- What do you think the company can improve at?
- How would you see yourself growing at this company in the next few years?
- Was there a time where you messed up and how was it handled?
- Why did you choose to come to this company?
- When you were last interviewing, what were some of your other options, and what made you choose this company?
- What was something you wish someone would have told you before you joined?
- What was your best moment so far at the company?

Cultural

- **What is the most frustrating part about working here?**
- **What is unique about working at this company that you have not experienced elsewhere?**

- What is something you wish were different about your job?
- How will the work I will be doing contribute to the organization's mission?
- What do you like about working here?
- What is your policy on working from home/remotely?
- (If the company is a startup) When was the last time you interacted with a founder? What was it regarding? Generally how involved are the founders in the day-to-day?
- Does the company culture encourage entrepreneurship? Could you give me any specific examples?

Technical

- **What are the engineering challenges that the company/team is facing?**
- **What has been the worst technical blunder that has happened in the recent past? How did you guys deal with it? What changes were implemented afterwards to make sure it didn't happen again?**
- **What is the most costly technical decision made early on that the company is living with now?**
- **What is the most fulfilling/exciting/technically complex project that you've worked on here so far?**
- **I do / don't have experience in domain X. How important is this for me to be able to succeed?**
- How do you evaluate new technologies? Who makes the final decisions?
- How do you know what to work on each day?
- How would you describe your engineering culture?
- How has your role changed since joining the company?

- What is your stack? What is the rationale for/story behind this specific stack?
- Do you tend to roll your own solutions more often or rely on third party tools? What's the rationale in a specific case?
- How does the engineering team balance resources between feature requests and engineering maintenance?
- What do you measure? What are your most important product metrics?
- What does the company do to nurture and train its employees?
- How often have you moved teams? What made you join the team you're on right now? If you wanted to move teams, what would need to happen?
- What resources does the company have for new hires to study its product and processes? Are there specifications, requirements, documentation?
- There's "C++" (or Python, Swift or any other tech) in the job description. How would you estimate my proficiency in this tech in 3 months?
- How do you think my expertise would be relevant to this team? What unique value can I add?

Product

- Tell me about the main products of your company.
- What is the current version of product? (If it is v1.0 or similar - there could be a lot of chaos to work with)
- What products are your main competitors?
- What makes your product competitive?
- When are you planning to provide the next release? (If in several months, it would mean a lot of requirements specified in job description are not needed right now)
- Is the team growing, and what sort of opportunities will there be in the next 3 years?

- What are your highest priorities right now? For example, new features, new products, solidifying existing code, reducing operations overhead?

Management

These questions are suitable for asking Engineering Managers, especially useful for the Team Matching phase of Google interviews or post-offer calls that your recruiters set up with the various team managers.

- **How do you train/ramp up engineers who are new to the team?**
- **What does success look like for your team/project?**
- **What qualities do you look out for when hiring for this role?**
- **What are the strengths and weaknesses of the current team? What is being done to improve upon the weaknesses?**
- **Can you tell me about a time you resolved an interpersonal conflict?**
- How did you become a manager?
- How do your engineers know what to work on each day?
- What is your team's biggest challenge right now?
- How do you measure individual performance?
- How often are 1:1s conducted?
- What is the current team composition like?
- What opportunities are available to switch roles? How does this work?
- Two senior team members disagree over a technical issue. How do you handle it?
- Have you managed a poor performer at some point in your career before? What did you do and how did it work?
- Where do you spend more of your time, with high performers or low performers?

- What is your management philosophy?
- What role does the manager play in making technical decisions?
- What is an example of a change you have made in the team that improved the team?
- What would be the most important problem you would want me to solve if I joined your team?
- What opportunities for growth will your team provide?
- What would I work on if I joined this team and who would I work most closely with?

Leadership

These questions are intended for senior level management, such as CEO, CTO, VPs. Candidates who interview with startups usually get to speak with senior level management.

- How are you funded?
- Are you profitable? If not, what's the plan for becoming profitable?
- What assurance do you have that this company will be successful?
- Tell me about your reporting structure.
- How does the company decide on what to work on next?

HR

- **How do you see this position evolving in the next three years?**
- **Who is your ideal candidate and how can I make myself more like them?**
- What concerns/reservations do you have about me for this position?
- What can I help to clarify that would make hiring me an easy decision?

- How does the management team deal with mistakes?
- If you could hire anyone to join your team, who would that be and why?
- How long does the average engineer stay at the company?
- Why have the last few people left?

References

- Business Insider
- Lifehacker
- Fastcompany
- Questions I'm asking in interviews
- How to interview your interviewers
- How to Break Into the Tech Industry—a Guide to Job Hunting and Tech Interviews
- A developer's guide to interviewing
- Questions I'm asking in interviews 2017
- What are good questions to ask during a software developer interview when asked "Do you have any questions now?"

Chapter 13 - Negotiation

Ten Rules of Negotiation

1. Get everything in writing

Note down *everything* on your phone call with the recruiters as small details might be helpful later on. Even if there are things that are not directly monetary, if they relate to the job, write them down. If they tell you *we're working on porting the front-end to Angular* write that down. If they say they have 20 employees, write it down. You want as much information as you can. You'll forget a lot of this stuff, and it's going to be important in informing your final decision.

2. Always keep the door open

Never give up your negotiating power until you are ready to make an informed, deliberate final decision. This means your job is to explore as many of these decision points as possible without giving up the power to continue the negotiation. Frequently, your interlocutor will try to trick you into making a decision, or tie you to a decision you didn't initially want to commit to. You must keep verbally jiu-jitsu-ing out of these antics until you're actually ready to make your final call.

3. Information is power

To keep the upper hand in the negotiation, you must protect information as much as possible. A corollary of this rule is that you should not reveal to companies what you're currently making. So given this offer, don't ask for more money or equity or anything of the sort. Don't comment on any specific details of the offer except to clarify them.

Companies will ask about your current compensation at different stages in the process, some before they ever interview you, some after they decide to make you an offer. But be mindful of this, and protect information.

> "Yes, that sounds great! I really thought this was a good fit, and I'm glad that you agree. Right now I'm talking with a few other companies so I can't speak to the specific details of the offer until I'm done with the process and get closer to making a decision. But I'm sure we'll be able to find a package that we're both happy with, because I really would love to be a part of the team."

4. Always be positive

Even if the offer is below your expectation, it's extremely important to remain positive and excited about the company. This is because your excitement is one of your most valuable assets in a negotiation.

Despite whatever is happening in the negotiation, give the company the impression that 1) you still like the company, and that 2) you're still excited to work there, even if the numbers or the money or the timing is not working out. Generally the most convincing thing to signal this is to reiterate you love the mission, the team, or the problem they're working on, and really want to see things work out.

5. Don't be the decision maker

Even if you don't particularly care what your friends/family/husband/mother thinks, by mentioning them, you're no longer the only person the recruiter needs to win over. There's no point in them trying to bully and intimidate you; the *true decision-maker* is beyond their reach.

This is a classic technique in customer support and remediation. It's never the person on the phone's fault, they're just some poor schmuck doing their job. It's not their decision to make. This helps to defuse tension and give them more control of the situation.

> I'll look over some of these details and discuss it with my [family/partner]. I'll reach out to you if I have any questions. Thanks so much for sharing the good news with me, and I'll be in touch!

It's much harder to pressure someone if they're not the final decision-maker. So take advantage of that.

6. Have alternatives

If you're already in the pipeline with other companies (which you should be if you're doing it right), you should proactively reach out and let them know that you've just received an offer. Try to build a sense of urgency. Regardless of whether you know the due date, all offers expire at some point, so take advantage of that.

> Hello [name],
>
> I just wanted to update you on my own process. I've just received an offer from [company] that is quite strong. That being said, I'm really excited about [your-amazing-company] and really want to see if we can make it work. Since my timeline is now tight, is there anything you can do to expedite the process?

Should you specifically mention the company that gave you an offer? Depends. If it's a well-known company or a competitor, then definitely mention it. If it's a no-name or unsexy company, you should just say you received an attractive offer. If it's expiring soon, you should mention that as well.

Either way, send out a letter like this to every single company you're talking to. No matter how hopeless or pointless you think your application is, you want to send them the signal that you are valued in the market.

Companies care that you've received other offers. They care because each company knows that their own process is noisy, and the processes of most other companies are also noisy. But a candidate having multiple offers means that they have multiple weak signals in their favor. Combined, these converge into a much stronger signal than any single interview. It's like knowing that a student has a strong SAT score, and GPA, and won various scholarships. Sure, it's still possible that they're a dunce, but it's much harder for that to be true.

This is not to say that companies respond proportionally to these signals, or that they don't overvalue credentials and brands. They do. But caring about whether you have other offers and valuing you accordingly is completely rational.

Your goal should be to have as many offers overlapping at the same time as possible. This will maximize your window for negotiating.

Have a strong BATNA (Best Alternative To a Negotiated Agreement) and communicate it.

> I've received another offer from [other-company] that's very compelling on salary, but I really love the mission of [your-company] and think that it would overall be a better fit for me. I'm also considering going back to grad school and getting a Master's degree in

Postmodern Haberdashery. I'm excited about [your-company] though and would love to join the team, but the package has to make sense.

7. Proclaim reasons for everything

It's kind of a brain-hack, both for yourself and for your negotiating partner. Just stating a reason (any reason) makes your request feel human and important. It's not you being greedy, it's you trying to fulfill your goals.

The more unobjectionable and sympathetic your reason, the better. If it's medical expenses, or paying off student loans, or taking care of family, you'll bring tears to their eyes.

Just go with it, state a reason for everything, and you'll find recruiters more willing to become your advocate.

8. Be motivated by more than just money

You should be motivated by money of course, but it should be one among many reasons you're after the given job. How much training you get, what will be your first project, which team will you join, or even who your mentor will be. These are all things you can and should negotiate.

Of course, to negotiate well, you need to understand the other side's perspective. You want to get the right deal better for both of you.

9. Understand what they value

Remember that you can always get pay raises as you continue to work at the company, but there's only one point at which you can get a signing bonus.

The easiest thing for a company to give though is stock (if the company offers stock). Companies like giving stock because it invests you in the company and aligns interests. It also shifts some of the risk from the company over to you and burns less cash.

10. Be winnable

This is more than just giving the company the impression that you like them (which you should). But more so that you must give any company you're talking to a clear path on how to win you. Don't bullshit them or play stupid games. Be clear and unequivocal with your preferences and timeline.

Don't waste their time or play games for your own purposes. Even if the company isn't your dream company, you must be able to imagine at least some package they could offer you that would make you sign. If not, politely turn them down fast.

References

Ten Rules for Negotiating a Job Offer

Chapter 14 - Interview Cheatsheet

This is a straight-to-the-point, distilled list of technical interview Do's and Don'ts, mainly for algorithmic interviews. Some of these may apply to only phone screens or whiteboard interviews, but most will apply to both. I read this list before each of my interviews to remind myself of the key points.

1. Before Interview

Prepare pen, paper and earphones/headphones.

Find a quiet environment with good Internet connection.

Ensure webcam and audio are working. There were times I had to restart Chrome to get Hangouts to work again.

Request for the option to interview over Hangouts/Skype instead of a phone call; it is easier to send links or text across.

Decide on and be familiar with a programming language.

Familiarize yourself with the coding environment (CoderPad/CodePen). Set up the coding shortcuts, turn on autocompletion, tab spacing, etc.

Prepare some questions to ask at the end of the interview.

Dress comfortably. Usually you do not need to wear smart clothes, casual should be fine. T-shirts and jeans are acceptable at most places.

Stay calm and composed.

2. Introduction

Introduce yourself in a few sentences under a minute or two.

Mention interesting points that are relevant to the role you are applying for.

Sound enthusiastic! Speak with a smile and you will naturally sound more engaging.

3. Upon Getting a Question

Repeat the question back at the interviewer.

Clarify any assumptions you made subconsciously. Many questions are under-specified on purpose. A tree-like diagram could very well be a graph that allows for cycles and a naive recursive solution would not work.

Clarify input format and range. Ask whether input can be assumed to be well-formed and non-null.

Work through a small example to ensure you understood the question.

Explain a high level approach even if it is a brute force one.

Improve upon the approach and optimize. Reduce duplicated work and cache repeated computations.

Think carefully, then state and explain the time and space complexity of your approaches.

If stuck, think about related problems you have seen before and how they were solved.

Don't ignore information given to you. Every piece is important.

Don't jump into coding straightaway.

Don't start coding without interviewer's green light.

Don't Appear too unsure about your approach or analysis.

4. During Coding

Explain what you are coding to the interviewer and what you are trying to achieve.

Practice good coding style. Meaningful variable names, consistent operator spacing, proper indentation, etc.

Type/write at a reasonable speed.

As much as possible, write actual compilable code, not pseudocode.

Write in a modular fashion. Extract out chunks of repeated code into functions.

Ask for permission to use trivial functions without having to implement them; saves you some time.

Keep in mind the hints given by the interviewer.

Demonstrate mastery of your chosen programming language.

Demonstrate technical knowledge in data structures and algorithms.

If you are cutting corners in your code, state that out loud to your interviewer and say what you would do in a non-interview setting (no time constraints). E.g., I would write a regex to parse this string rather than using split() which may not cover all cases.

Practice whiteboard space-management skills.

Don't remain quiet the whole time.

Don't spend too much time writing comments.

Don't use extremely verbose variable names.

Don't interrupt your interviewer when they are talking. Usually if they speak, they are trying to give you hints or steer you in the right direction.

Don't write too big (takes up too much space) or too small (illegible).

5. After Coding

Scan through your code for mistakes as if it was your first time seeing code written by someone else.

Check for off-by-one errors.

Come up with more test cases. Try extreme test cases.

Step through your code with those test cases.

Look out for places where you can refactor.

Reiterate the time and space complexity of your code.

Explain trade-offs and how the code can be improved if given more time.

Don't immediately announce that you are done coding. Do the above first!

Don't argue with the interviewer. They may be wrong but that is very unlikely given that they are familiar with the question.

6. Wrapping Up

Ask questions. More importantly, ask good and engaging questions that are tailored to the company.

Thank the interviewer.

Don't ask about your interview performance. It can get awkward.

Don't end the interview without asking any questions.

7. Post Interview

Record the interview questions and answers down as these can be useful for future reference.

Send a follow up email to your interviewer(s) thanking them for their time and the opportunity to interview with them.

Appendix

Flat access to all URLs

If you are reading this on the Kindle or got a hard copy, you can conveniently type this shortlink on your browser to see all the exercises and further reading reference links: https://bit.ly/2Eh45fM or https://tinyurl.com/yacn99hb

Practice your SQL

Practice and improve your SQL skills on SQLBOLT

All LeetCode exercises

- LRU cache
- sliding window technique

Practice Math Online

- Pow(x, n)
- Sqrt(x)
- Integer to English Words

Practice Binary Online

- Sum of Two Integers
- Number of 1 Bits
- Counting Bits
- Missing Number
- Reverse Bits

Practice Arrays Online

- Two Sum
- Best Time to Buy and Sell Stock

- Contains Duplicate
- Product of Array Except Self
- Maximum Subarray
- Maximum Product Subarray
- Find Minimum in Rotated Sorted Array
- Search in Rotated Sorted Array
- 3Sum
- Container With Most Water

Practice String Online

- Longest Substring Without Repeating Characters
- Longest Repeating Character Replacement
- Minimum Window Substring
- Valid Anagram
- Group Anagrams
- Valid Parentheses
- Valid Palindrome
- Longest Palindromic Substring
- Palindromic Substrings

Practice Interval Online

- Insert Interval
- Merge Intervals
- Non-overlapping Intervals

Practice Graph Online

- Clone Graph
- Course Schedule
- Pacific Atlantic Water Flow
- Number of Islands
- Longest Consecutive Sequence

Practice Matrix Online

- Set Matrix Zeroes
- Spiral Matrix
- Rotate Image
- Word Search

Practice Linked Lists Online

- Reverse a Linked List
- Detect Cycle in a Linked List
- Merge Two Sorted Lists
- Merge K Sorted Lists
- Remove Nth Node From End Of List
- Reorder List

Practice Tree Online

- Maximum Depth of Binary Tree
- Same Tree
- Invert/Flip Binary Tree
- Binary Tree Maximum Path Sum
- Binary Tree Level Order Traversal
- Serialize and Deserialize Binary Tree
- Subtree of Another Tree
- Construct Binary Tree from Preorder and Inorder Traversal
- Validate Binary Search Tree
- Kth Smallest Element in a BST
- Lowest Common Ancestor of BST

Practice Trie Online

- Implement Trie (Prefix Tree)
- Add and Search Word
- Word Search II

Practice Heap Online

- Merge K Sorted Lists
- Top K Frequent Elements
- Find Median from Data Stream

Practice Recursion Online

- Subsets and Subsets II

Practice Dynamic Programming Online

- Climbing Stairs
- Coin Change
- Longest Increasing Subsequence
- Word Break Problem
- Combination Sum
- House Robber and House Robber II
- Decode Ways
- Unique Paths
- Jump Game

Further Studies Online

- Bits, Bytes, Building With Binary
- Demystifying Dynamic Programming
- Dynamic Programming – 7 Steps to Solve any DP Interview Problem
- From Theory To Practice: Representing Graphs
- Deep Dive Through A Graph: DFS Traversal
- Going Broad In A Graph: BFS Traversal
- Leaf It Up To Binary Trees
- Trying to Understand Tries
- Implement Trie (Prefix Tree)
- Learning to Love Heaps

All Online Solutions

Typical Math Questions

1. Given a string such as "123" or "67", write a function to output the number represented by the string without using casting. (Solution)
2. Make a program that can print out the text form of numbers from 1 to 9999 (ex. 20 is "twenty", 105 is "one hundred and five", 2655 is "two thousand six undred fifty five). (Solution)
3. How would you convert Roman numerals into decimals? E.g. XIV becomes 14. (Solution)
4. Compute the square root of an Integer without using any existing built in math functions. (Solution)

Typical Binary Interview Questions

1. How do you verify if an integer is a power of 2? (Solution)
2. Write a program to print the binary representation of an integer. (Solution)
3. Write a program to print out the number of 1 bits in a given integer. (Solution)
4. Write a program to determine the next higher integer using the same number of 1 bits in a given number. (Solution)

Typical Arrays Interview Questions

1. Given an array and an index, find the product of the elements of the array except the element at that index. (Solution)
2. Given 2 separate arrays, write a method to find the values that exist in both arrays and return them. (Solution)
3. Given an array of numbers, list out all triplets that sum to 0. Do so with a running time of less than $O(n^3)$. (Solution 1)
4. Given an array of integers, find the subarray with the largest sum. (Solution)

5. Find the second maximum value in an array. (Solution)
6. Remove duplicates in an unsorted array where the duplicates are at a distance of k or less from each other. (Solution)
7. Given an unsorted list of integers, return true if the list contains any duplicates within k indices of each element. Do it faster than O(n^2). (Solution)
8. Given an array of string, find the duplicated elements. (Solution)
9. Given an array of integers, modify the array by moving all the zeroes to the end (right side). The order of other elements doesn't matter. E.g. [1, 2, 0, 3, 0, 1, 2], the program could output [1, 2, 3, 1, 2, 0, 0]. (Solution)
10. Given an array of integers where every value appears twice except one, find the single, non-repeating value. Follow up: do so with O(1) space. E.g., [2, 5, 3, 2, 1, 3, 4, 5, 1] returns 4, because it is the only value that appears in the array only once. (Solution)

Typical String Interview Questions

1. Write a program that checks if a sentence is palindrome or not. You can ignore white spaces and other characters to consider sentence as a palindrome. (Solution)
2. Given a list of words, find if any of the two words can be joined to form a palindrome. (Solution)
3. Write a functions that returns true if edit distance between two strings is one. An edit is characterised by either a character add, remove, or change in the string. (Solution)
4. How would you define a spell-checking algorithm? (Solution)
5. Given a string, return the string with duplicate characters removed. (Solution)

6. Given a rectangular grid with letters, search if some word is in the grid. (Solution)
7. Given two numbers as strings. The numbers may be very large (may not fit in long long int), the task is to find the sum of these two numbers. (Solution)
8. Find the longest palindrome in a string. (Solution)
9. Check whether two strings are anagram of each other. (Solution)
10. Run length encoding - Given an input string, write a function that returns the Run Length Encoded string for the input string. For example, if the input string is "wwwwaaadexxxxxx", then the function should return "w4a3d1e1x6". (Solution)
11. Given a dictionary find out if given word can be made by two words in the dictionary. (Solution)

Typical Interval Interview questions

1. Consider a big party where a log register for guest's entry and exit times is maintained. Find the time at which there are maximum guests in the party. Note that entries in register are not in any order. (Solution)
2. Given a set of time intervals in any order, merge all overlapping intervals into one and output the result which should have only mutually exclusive intervals. Let the intervals be represented as pairs of integers for simplicity. (Solution)
3. Given a set of non-overlapping intervals and a new interval, insert the interval at correct position. If the insertion results in overlapping intervals, then merge the overlapping intervals. Assume that the set of non-overlapping intervals is sorted on the basis of start time, to find correct position of insertion. (Solution)
4. Given n appointments, find all conflicting appointments. e.g appointments: [1, 5] [3, 7], [2, 6],

257

{10, 15}, {5, 6}, {4, 100} should output:

- [3,7] Conflicts with [1,5]
- [2,6] Conflicts with [1,5]
- [5,6] Conflicts with [3,7]
- [4,100] Conflicts with [1,5] (Solution)

Typical Graph Interview Questions

1. Given a list of sorted words from an alien dictionary, find the order of the alphabet. (Solution)
2. Given a graph and two nodes, determine if there exists a path between them. (Solution)
3. Determine if a cycle exists in a directed graph. (Solution)

Typical Matrix Interview Questions

1. Given a 4 x 4 matrix, the task is to interchange the elements of the first and last column and show the resulting matrix. (Solution)
2. Boggle implementation. Given a dictionary, and a matrix of letters, find all the words in the matrix that are in the dictionary. You can go across, down or diagonally. (Solution)
3. Given a 2D array, print it in spiral form. (Solution)

Typical Linked List Interview Questions

1. Write a SortedMerge() function that takes two lists, each of which is sorted in increasing order, and merges the two together into one list which is in increasing order. (Solution)
2. Implement an LRU cache with O(1) runtime for all its operations. (Solution)
3. Given a singly linked list (a list which can only be traversed in one direction), find the item that is

located at k items from the end. So if the list is a, b, c, d and k is 2 then the answer is c. The solution should not search the list twice. (Solution)
4. How can you tell if a Linked List is a Palindrome? (Solution)

Typical Tree Interview Questions

1. Find the height of a binary tree. (Solution)
2. Find the deepest left leaf of a binary tree. (Solution)
3. Given the roots of a tree. print out all of its root-to-leaf paths one per line. (Solution)
4. Given a binary tree, print level order traversal in a way that nodes of all levels are printed in separate lines. (Solution)
5. Determine if a binary tree is "complete" (i.e, if all leaf nodes were either at the maximum depth or max depth-1, and were 'pressed' along the left side of the tree). (Solution)
6. Determine if a binary tree is a BST. (Solution)
7. Given a binary tree, serialize it into a string. Then deserialize it. (Solution)
8. Given a node, find the next element in a BST. (Solution)
9. Pretty print a JSON object. (Solution)
10. Convert a binary tree to a doubly circular linked list. (Solution)
11. Find the second largest number in a binary tree. (Solution)
12. Convert a tree to a linked list. (Solution)
13. Find the Deepest node in a Binary tree.(Solution

Typical Heap Interview Questions

1. Merge K sorted lists together into a single list. (Solution)

2. Given a stream of integers, write an efficient function that returns the median value of the integers. (Solution)

Typical Recursion Interview Questions

1. Given two number x and y find their product using recursion (Solution)
2. Given a number, write a function that returns the sum of its digits using recursion. e.g "1234" should return 10. (Solution)

Typical Dynamic Programming Interview questions

1. There are N stations on route of a train. The train goes from station 0 to N-1. The ticket cost for all pair of stations (i, j) is given where j is greater than i. Find the minimum cost to reach the destination. (Solution)
2. Given N friends, each one can remain single or can be paired up with some other friend. Each friend can be paired only once. Find out the total number of ways in which friends can remain single or can be paired up. (Solution)

Table Of Contents

Appendix